PILLARS
OF THE
CHRISTIAN
faith

DANNY SHELTON - JIM GILLEY

Remnant
Publications

Coldwater MI 49036
www.remnantpublications.com

Copy editing by Debi Tesser & Tarah Benton
Cover design by Chrystique Neibauer | cqgraphicdesign.com
Text design by Greg Solie • AltamontGraphics.com

ISBN 978-1-933291-48-2

Table of Contents

Preface

I t makes sense, doesn't it, that God would have a special message of truth to give to the entire world just before He returns?

"Then I saw another angel flying in the midst of heaven, having the everlasting gospel to preach to those who dwell on the earth—to every nation, tribe, tongue, and people—saying with a loud voice, 'Fear God and give glory to Him, for the hour of His judgment has come; and worship Him who made heaven and earth, the sea and springs of water.'" (Revelation 14:6, 7)

This message—"present truth" as it has been called by many—is timely yet timeless. It's the "everlasting gospel." Also, this message of truth—a call back to the truths of God's Word and a specific warning to those who stubbornly refuse to accept His truth—is going to be given to the entire world just before He returns to this earth.

The night I received the clear impression from the Lord that I was to build a television station to reach the entire world with a message, it was clear what that message was to be: "the undiluted three angels' messages." I actually had to look up this phrase in Revelation to find out what it was. Of course, I had heard of it, but I did not know what it was specifically until I read Revelation 14:6-13. So it was for the very purpose of declaring this end-time message that Three Angels Broadcasting Network came into existence—and it's the reason it continues.

My coauthor, Jim Gilley, had a similar experience several years earlier. Jim had completed college and seminary and had spent a short time as a pastor. Then when he was only 25 years old, he became a conference evangelist. Jim had grown up in a family of small-business people. His grandmother, widowed at a young age, had built a successful awning and drapery company. She had six daughters and one son, Jim's dad. Jim had that same entrepreneurial spirit and moved to another city and started a business as well.

Jim had these genes, so he dreamed of a ministry that he would support with his own business. He had started a business when barely out of his teens that had sustained him and his wife, Camille, as they finished their education at Andrews University. He sold that business (which still exists in Berrien Springs, Michigan) when he entered the ministry.

Jim returned to Dallas, Texas, where he had lived as a teenager, to begin a business career with the intentions of doing ministry, but he became completely side-tracked until, providentially, he was led to purchase a business more compatible with ministry. The impression that he should begin a television ministry came, and though his plans were derailed, he began to hold evangelistic meetings again. Starting with small meetings, God blessed his ministry, and he held more than fifty full-length evangelistic series as an ASI member who combined business with evangelism before returning to full-time ministry and eventually joining me at 3ABN.

So we are both dedicated to presenting this Bible truth and have been for many years.

You might ask me, "Why do you believe in the Bible?" This is a short book, not a full library, so I am going to give you short answers to many of your questions, but I will also tell you where to find more in-depth answers to your questions, for those who may need them.

One reason I believe in the Bible is Daniel, the second chapter. Nebuchadnezzar had a dream, and none of his wise men could interpret it until Daniel was called (Daniel 2:24–49). In this dream of the image of metal and mud, God outlined the kingdoms that would rule the world.

Babylon was the head of gold, which was ruling at the time. The chest and arms of silver represented Media-Persia, which was to overthrow Babylon. The belly and thighs of bronze represented Greece; the legs of iron represented the iron monarchy of Rome; and the feet of iron and clay represented the kingdoms of Europe, combined with Rome. This is the history of the world written in advance. Each of these kingdoms ruled exactly as predicted by prophecy.

In addition, all of the Bible writers and Jesus Christ our Lord—the focus of the entire New Testament—all believed it. So in accepting the Word of God by faith, I am in very good company.

What does the Bible claim to be? Let's open the Word and let it speak for itself. First, it claims to be inspired by God. "All Scripture is given by inspiration of God" (2 Timothy 3:16). The authors never claimed authorship—they gave all the credit to God.

Next, the Bible claims to have been written by men who were inspired by the Holy Ghost. "For prophecy never came by the will of man, but holy men of God spoke as they were moved by the Holy Spirit" (2 Peter 1:21).

Finally, in the Old Testament, we read: "The Spirit of the Lord spoke by me, and His word was on my tongue" (2 Samuel 23:2).

The Holy Ghost, or Holy Spirit, represents God to all people everywhere upon this earth. God is omnipresent through His Holy Spirit. This same Spirit guided the Bible writers in all that they wrote.

Until this past century, little was known about some of the civilizations of the past, except from the biblical account. This caused some ancient historians to doubt the biblical account of history. For instance, at that time no one understood the hieroglyphics—the ancient writing of Egypt. Then in 1798, Napoleon Bonaparte led a military expedition into Egypt. In addition to 38,000 soldiers, he took 100 artists, linguists, and scientists with him. They saw the mysterious relics of the past with decorated walls, and they wondered what it meant.

A year later, in 1799, an unassuming soldier unearthed a very unusual, large black stone about four feet by two-and-a-half feet near the town of Rosetta in Egypt. It became known as the Rosetta Stone, which is now in London's British Museum. The stone revealed an ancient decree in three different scripts—Greek, Egyptian, and hieroglyphic picture writing.

The Egyptian and the Greek were quickly translated, but not until twenty years later did a French scholar break the hieroglyphic code. This opened up the extensive writings of the Egyptians that gave great insights into their history and confirmed the biblical account.

Other discoveries, such as the Dead Sea Scrolls and the Ebla Tablets— a whole library dating back to the time of Moses—revealed accounts of Creation and the Flood, as well as names, places, and events that previously had only been found in the Bible. They also mentioned the destruction of Sodom and Gomorrah.

Some critics had claimed that the Scriptures had been changed, but the Dead Sea Scrolls confirmed that the Scriptures that Jesus Christ read in the synagogue were the same Scriptures we have today. So you can have confidence in the Word of God.

—Danny Shelton

Introduction

Our hope and prayer is that after reading this book in the *Pillars of Our Faith* series, you will want more than ever to "dare to be a Daniel"—and, like him, stand tall for truth.

An old saying says: "If you don't stand for something, you will fall for anything." Sadly, many Christians today are falling for Satan's lies and will ultimately lose out on the free gift of salvation because they choose not to put on the armor of God and stand for truth.

The Christian faith is built on the firm belief that Jesus Christ is the Creator and Redeemer of the human race. Since He is our Creator, it is our belief—substantiated by the Bible—that we are "not our own" and that "we are bought with a price" (1 Corinthians 6:19, 20 KJV).

God created us to live forever as explained to us in the book of Genesis. But when Adam and Eve fell into sin, their sin separated them from God so that they could no longer live forever. Either the human race would end in the Garden of Eden, or God would have to make a way to save the people He had made.

Thankfully, God loved them so much that He came up with a plan to allow every human being ever to be born into sin a way of escape. That plan, of course, we call the plan of salvation. Nowhere in the Bible is it described more simply and beautifully than in John 3:16: "For God so loved the world, that he gave his only begotten Son, that whosoever believeth in him should not perish, but have everlasting life" (KJV).

Yes, a plan of redemption for fallen man!

While this book addresses this great sacrifice by the Godhead, it also addresses a real here-and-now problem. Let's let the Bible describe it as found in John 10:10: "The thief [Satan] cometh not, but for to steal, and to kill, and to destroy: I am come that they might have life, and that they might have it more abundantly" (KJV).

Praise God! There it is—a plan of escape from our own deserved death to life everlasting, through the death of Jesus Christ as a substitute for every sinner.

This book that you hold in your hands targets mainly those who have accepted Jesus Christ as Lord and Savior at one time or another. But we invite all who want a better understanding of Jesus Christ and His plan to redeem fallen man to join with us in seeking for answers to why spiritual erosion seems to be making its mark on virtually every church, regardless of the name over the doorpost.

We think most readers will affirm the book called the Bible as our only road map to find a true understanding of our loving Creator God. Contained in the Bible is a set of laws called the Ten Commandments. God gave this law to His people as a guideline for a healthy, happy life here on earth. The story of God giving the Ten Commandments to Moses is found in Exodus, the twentieth chapter. Many believe that these laws were introduced for the first time when given to the Jewish nation there on Mt. Sinai.

The truth is, the Ten Commandments are as old as the creation of Planet Earth, and in reality they date back as far as God Himself—the Alpha and Omega—who had no beginning and will have no end.

Why? The Ten Commandments are in reality like an exact photograph of God's own character of love. Heaven has been governed by these laws forever, and it wasn't until Satan chose to rebel against God and His eternal laws of love and peace that the inhabitants of unfallen worlds throughout the universe could see the terrible results of what is now termed "sin."

For just a quick refresher, let's turn to the Bible and find out what sin really is: "Sin is the transgression [breaking] of the law" (1 John 3:4 KJV).

The Bible records in Isaiah that Satan purposed in his heart to be like the most high God—thus, sin entered into this world. We just read where the Bible says that sin is the transgression of the law. So a fair question would be: "If God's law is transgressed or broken, what will the results be for the person transgressing it?" Once again, we turn to the Bible to find the truth: "The wages of sin is death; but the gift of God is eternal life through Jesus Christ our Lord" (Romans 6:23 KJV). Amazing! According to the Bible, the breaking of God's laws will result in death.

Because God loves us so much, He came up with a plan of redemption to save us from this inevitable death. A great controversy has been going on between Christ and Satan for more than 6,000 years now—yes, a controversy about ownership of the whole human race that began before Creation. Satan says that because human beings chose to follow him in the Garden of Eden when they ate the forbidden fruit, all of them should suffer eternal death.

God claims that the human race belongs to Him because not only is He their Creator but also their Redeemer through His Son, Jesus Christ—who came to earth in human form and overcame death, hell, and the grave by living a sinless life. Christ's death transferred the sins of the human race to our Savior, Jesus Christ, giving every human ever born on this sinful planet a way of escape.

Satan does not have the power to kill God, so he has turned his focus—as John 10:10 says—to killing humanity. This book you are reading exposes Satan's plan of deception to accomplish his end.

Satan is the father of lies and the master deceiver. The good news is that Satan's days are numbered.

We contend that deception is a choice! Let us explain. If we submit and commit our lives to God and stay close to Him by living up to all the light of truth we have, God is able to put a hedge about us that will keep us out of the grasp of Satan.

We've already briefly described God's plan of redemption for the human race. This book will clearly expose Satan's plan for the destruction of mankind. Thus, the title of this book is *Pillars of the Christian Faith.*

Satan's plan of deception is unmasked in these pages as we describe in considerable detail his plans to chip away at the very foundation and pillars of the Christian faith, sometimes even using unsuspecting professed followers of Christ to do his bidding.

—Jim Gilley

CHAPTER 1

Did God Create Both Good and Evil?

A t some point after we're born, questions arise for each of us:
"Who am I?"
"How did I get here?"
"How did this world around me get here?"

Those around us—parents, teachers, preachers, and others—have answers for us. Some tell us we evolved from monkeys and apes over millions of years, which in turn evolved from lower forms of life. Others say the questions don't matter—that we should just enjoy life while we can while we're here. We also learn soon enough that a certain book—the Bible—claims that human beings, Earth itself, and the entire universe, are the creations of God.

So the choice confronts each of us: What shall we do about the question of how we got here? Who should we believe?

Some just choose to ignore the question. But most of us really want to know. Are we just the latest and most advanced primates on earth—the result of millions if not billions of years of evolution? Or is the Bible true, and God did indeed create the human race?

In this chapter, we're going to focus on this second option—that God created not only human beings and the earth on which we live but also the entire universe.

The Bible begins with the Genesis account of six days of Creation. To accept what Genesis says requires a choice of faith. That faith is not blind but intelligent, and it rests on evidence.

Some have asked me, "What did Moses know about Creation?" Moses wrote the Genesis account, and I believe the same God who gave Moses the Ten Commandments revealed to him the Creation story in Genesis.

Throughout the Old Testament, we find stated over and over again that God created the earth. Also, in the New Testament we find that the active member of the Godhead in Creation was Jesus Christ, which gave Him the right to be our Savior. John began his Gospel with these words: "In the beginning was the Word, and the Word was with God, and the Word was God. He was in the beginning with God. All things were made through Him, and without Him nothing was made that was made" (John 1:1-3).

So John told us that Jesus is the Word, that He has no beginning, that He is God, and that He is the Creator.

Notice this too in 1 Corinthians 10:3, 4: "All ate the same spiritual food, and all drank the same spiritual drink. For they drank of that spiritual Rock that followed them, and that Rock was Christ."

Can you imagine it? The "Bread of Life," Jesus, is the one who fed the children of Israel the manna that was provided to them six days each week—with a double portion on the sixth day so that they could remember on the Sabbath. Yes, that God, their Creator and Provider, was Jesus Himself.

New Testament texts that point out that Jesus Christ is the Creator God are numerous. Here are just a few:

- "God who created all things through Jesus Christ" (Ephesians 3:9).

- "For by Him [Christ] all things were created that are in heaven and that are on earth, visible and invisible, whether thrones or dominions or principalities or powers. All things were created through Him and for Him" (Colossians 1:16).

- "God, who at various times and in various ways spoke in time past to the fathers by the prophets, has in these last days spoken to us by His Son, whom He has appointed heir of all things, through whom also He made the worlds" (Hebrews 1:1, 2).

So clearly, if any of us refuses to believe in the Genesis account of Creation, that means we must then deny the divinity of Christ. And that would mean we must also deny that He has the power to save us and all who will accept Him as their Savior from sin. Do you see why this way of thinking could become a slippery slope?

Another slippery slope is to conclude that God created not only all good things—but the bad ones too. Some ask, "If the Bible is true, and God created this world, did He also create the sin and suffering we see around us?" That's a good and fair question, and one for which the Bible gives us a clear answer.

Sin did get its start in heaven, but sin was not started by God but by one of His created beings, Lucifer.

Some would yet ask, "Did God create Lucifer with a sinful nature?" The Bible gives us the answer in verse 15 of Ezekiel 28: "You [Lucifer] were perfect in your ways from the day you were created, till iniquity was found in you."

You see, God didn't create the devil. No, he created Lucifer, "son of the morning," the anointed one, the most highly ranked angel in all of heaven—but Lucifer turned himself into the devil.

So you might say, "Wait a minute—if God created a being with the ability to become the devil, then God created the devil." No, that isn't true. You see, God could have created all beings, including you and me, so that we *could not* sin. But if He had done that, He could not have created us in His image, could he? He created us with the ability to make a decision—to make choices. He gave us the ability to love and obey or to hate and disobey—to have a free will. Throughout eternity, no angel had ever sinned, and no being had ever questioned God. But then Lucifer questioned God, and he sinned when he used the free choice God gave him to choose against God. At that point God had a real challenge on His hands.

Why did Lucifer sin?

"Your heart was lifted up because of your beauty; you corrupted your wisdom for the sake of your splendor; I cast you to the ground, I laid you before kings, that they might gaze at you." (Ezekiel 28:17)

Lucifer's beauty and wisdom grew that pride in his heart, and that caused him to make the step away from God. Pride is still the basis of all sin, even today.

Heaven is going to be filled with people God can trust, and that brings to mind some very important questions to ask yourself: "Can God trust me?" "Can God *really* trust me?" "If I ever had the same choice as Lucifer had, would I try what he tried to do—to take God's place?" Yes, it was a ridiculous choice for Lucifer to make. Just look at all of the trouble it has caused.

The Bible says that Lucifer wanted to be God. Verse 14 of Isaiah 14 says that he told himself: "I will ascend above the heights of the clouds, I will be like the Most High."

Lucifer did not desire the character of God—to be like Him in His goodness—which we all should imitate. He wanted the power and position of God. He wanted to be worshiped. "I'm going to be like the Most High," he said. And he reached for a higher place, but he reached too far. He forgot that he was created and not the Creator—and there's a very big difference.

The Bible tells us more about the character of Lucifer since, you see, Lucifer began to talk against God to all the angels of heaven. The amazing thing was, as the Bible tells us, that one-third of the angels of heaven joined him, and they were cast out as well. That's a large number. He was very persuasive, wasn't he?

However, I've often heard it asked, "Why didn't God just wipe out Lucifer and his angels right then and bring sin to an end?"

God still had two-thirds of the angels left, looking on. If there are other inhabited worlds in the universe—and the Bible seems to indicate that there are—they too would be looking on. If God had destroyed Satan and his angels right then, that would have raised a lot of questions. In the future all beings would serve Him out of fear and not out of love.

Sometimes we think we know better than God how the sin problem should have been handled. How amazingly arrogant of us! God knows best, and we will see when it is all over that He made the right decision in letting sin run its course, painful as that may have been at the moment.

Lucifer had been lying about God. What does the Bible say about him in John, chapter 8, verse 44? "You are of your father the devil, and the desires of your father you want to do. He was a murderer from the beginning, and does not stand in the truth, because there is no truth in him. When he speaks a lie, he speaks from his own resources, for he is a liar and the father of it."

Lucifer could take something and turn it—spin it as we would say to-day—just a little, but truth then became a lie. God has said that Satan is a liar and the father of it, and he lied about God. Have you ever had someone lie about you? Sometimes, even when you prove it isn't true, some people continue to have lingering doubts, don't they? Unfortunately, once questions were raised about God, doubts set in.

So then, what could God do? He could reason with the angels, and I'm sure that He did. He could talk to them and say, "Look at My record throughout eternity, and you will see that I am a God of love who has stood always for that which is right and true."

But here's Lucifer, now the devil, and he has said and continues to say, "No, God is a tyrant, and His law is against us. We've got to do something. We need freedom from His law, so we can all be gods."

How should God respond? I am sure He exhausted all options. He could reason and persuade, but in time, the rebellion came to a head. We find the result in Revelation 12:7: "War broke out in heaven: Michael and his angels fought with the dragon; and the dragon and his angels fought."

Further, verse 9 tells us the result of that war: "The great dragon was cast out, that serpent of old, called the Devil and Satan, who deceives the whole world; he was cast to the earth, and his angels were cast out with him."

After being ejected from heaven, Satan was on this newly created planet. But the conflict between God and Satan was not over. The battle that had begun in heaven had simply moved to earth. The next thing Satan did was to involve the newly created occupants of this world, Adam and Eve. They were tempted, and tragically, they fell for the same basic line that had brought down a third of the angels of heaven—that God was trying to keep something good from them. "God knows that in the day you eat of it your eyes will be opened, and you will be like God, knowing good and evil" (Genesis 3:5).

Satan had wanted to take the place of God. So he told Eve that she could be a god if she would just do what God had told her she should not do. God had also told Adam and Eve that if they disobeyed, they would die (Genesis 2:17). But Satan lied and told Eve that she wouldn't die (Genesis 3:4). Our first parents chose not to believe God and to disobey Him, which brought sin and death into this world. So often today, we still buy Satan's lies instead of the truth of God's Word.

But God had anticipated the fall of mankind, and His only Son—a member of the Trinity composed of the Father, Son, and Holy Spirit, all fully equal in all ways—volunteered to come to this earth. He would come to show us what God is truly like and to die on the cross, paying the penalty for the sins of mankind and giving eternal life to all who accept Him. This is the "everlasting gospel" that we read about in Revelation 14:6. It's the plan of salvation, so clearly stated in John 3:16: "For God so loved the world that He gave His only begotten Son, that whoever believes in Him should not perish but have everlasting life."

Yes, God will put an end to sin and suffering. Satan will be destroyed: "All who knew you among the peoples are astonished at you; you have become a horror, and shall be no more forever" (Ezekiel 28:19).

But God will save all who accept the saving blood of His Son, Jesus. As Paul said, in 2 Corinthians 9:15: "Thanks be to God for His indescribable gift!"

God will restore this earth to its original perfect condition and bring an end to sin and suffering forever. As the Bible says in Revelation 21:4: "God will wipe away every tear from their eyes; there shall be no more death, nor sorrow, nor crying. There shall be no more pain, for the former things have passed away."

I so look forward to that, don't you? I believe that God will do just exactly what He says He will do. No, God is not sitting off in the distance, untouched by sin. Heaven was more than touched, when one-third of its inhabitants fell, and they were cast out with Satan. Still, God's own family was touched when His Son Jesus died on the cross. So you can trust Him

CHAPTER 2

Traveling through Time

Time travel is a fascinating interest for many. Books and movies have explored it. Scientists speculate about whether or not it's possible. What about you? If you could travel through time, would you want to do it? Would you choose to go back in time? If so, to what year or time period? Or would you choose to go into the future? And if so, again, how far?

The Bible, as it turns out, offers its own form of time travel—we call it prophecy. It opens windows into what will happen in the future. The longest leap through time described in the Bible is a long one indeed!

But before we explore that time prophecy, we need first to look at one of the great topics of the three angels' messages of Revelation 14—the topic of judgment.

So to begin, come back with me to the trial—the judgment—of Jesus. Yes, they had a trial, but it was not a legal trial, as it was taking place at an hour when it could not legally take place. Though a sham, it was a trial. They found Him guilty, when He was innocent. They put Him on a cross, He died, and then He came forth three days later from the tomb.

However, there is to be another trial that captures the attention of the entire universe, just as the sham trial of Jesus did before His crucifixion. This time, the trial will be conducted by the Supreme Court of the entire universe. This one will be a legal trial, and the Judge, the Bible tells us, will be Jesus Himself. This trial is spoken of throughout all of Scripture—it is called the great white throne judgment.

> "For we must all appear before the judgment seat of Christ, that each one may receive the things done in the body, according to what he has done, whether good or bad." (2 Corinthians 5:10)

"And do you think this, O man, you who judge those practicing such things, and doing the same, that you will escape the judgment of God?" (Romans 2:3)

I don't suppose anything is worse than someone who does wrong but stands in judgment of others. Not one of us has ever lived a perfect life, and if we stand in judgment of other people, God says to us, "Listen, you are going to stand in the judgment day, and you are going to answer for that—judge not, lest you be judged."

There's going to be a judgment, and you can be assured that judgment is going to take place. In fact, the Bible speaks of it, and it is already taking place. A lot of people think they are assured of salvation in that judgment, but the Bible says that not everyone who claims Christ will be saved.

"Many will say to Me in that day, 'Lord, Lord, have we not prophesied in Your name, cast out demons in Your name, and done many wonders in Your name?' And then I will declare to them, 'I never knew you; depart from Me, you who practice lawlessness!'" (Matthew 7:22, 23)

Works—"being good"—will not save you. God says that in the judgment some will say, "Look at me! I was doing wonderful works during my lifetime. I was doing everything I could for you. I was paying a tenth of my income. I was giving another tenth for offerings. And I was getting involved in every good thing possible."

But an ingredient was missing. That person had not been covered by the blood of the Lamb of God, Jesus Christ. The Bible says that Jesus will say to them, "Depart from me, you who work iniquity" (Matthew 7:23 KJV).

Even though they may have many wonderful works to which they can point, God says that's not any indicator at all. You might be some well-known television preacher, or you might even perform miracles and cast out devils in front of thousands of people, but God says that doesn't necessarily indicate that you're going to be able to stand in that judgment. That makes the judgment serious, doesn't it? That means that we really need to take a careful look at what the Bible says about this.

"I saw the dead, small and great, standing before God, and books were opened. And another book was opened, which is the Book of Life. And the dead were judged according to their works, by the things which were written in the books." (Revelation 20:12)

The Bible says not only the living but those who have died are going to be judged. It talks about the dead being judged from those books in heaven. Now notice this awesome Bible picture of the judgment scene:

"I watched till thrones were put in place, and the Ancient of Days was seated; His garment was white as snow, and the hair of His head was like pure wool. His throne was a fiery flame, its wheels a burning fire; a fiery stream issued and came forth from before Him. A thousand thousands ministered to Him; ten thousand times ten thousand stood before Him. The court was seated, and the books were opened." (Daniel 7:9, 10)

The judgment was set. The books were opened, and that great white throne judgment began. It seems to me that the Bible speaks very clearly on this subject.

But now, let's finally consider that great time-travel prophecy mentioned as this chapter began. An angel helped the prophet Daniel understand a vision he saw: "And he said to me, 'For two thousand three hundred days; then the sanctuary shall be cleansed'" (Daniel 8:14).

Every year in old Israel, the Day of Atonement took place—a day of judgment that involved the cleansing of the sanctuary. It always took place on the tenth day of the seventh month of the Jewish year. Every year the exact time was set. The Bible tells us that God also had an exact time when He began to sit as Judge in the final judgment.

We could talk at length about the Old Testament sanctuary and all of the furniture in it. At first, the sanctuary traveled with Israel in the wilderness. Later, they took all of its contents—the furniture, a veil, everything—and placed it all in the temple. If you were just to look at all the contents in the sanctuary, you would find that every single item in it—and every service conducted in it—pointed to Jesus Christ.

Consider the ark. No, not "Noah's ark"—this was the ark of the covenant—and it was in the Most Holy Place of the sanctuary. Inside that ark there were three items:

- The tablets of stone—the Ten Commandments—written by the very finger of God.

- Aaron's rod—the one that budded, even though it was dead, representing the death and resurrection of Jesus Christ.

- A bowl of manna—both a reminder of how God had fed Israel in the wilderness and of Jesus, the Bread of Life.

Every single thing in the sanctuary represented Jesus Christ. His death for you and for me was represented by the sacrifice of a lamb—an object lesson pointing forward to the cross. Now that we who live after the cross have seen it, we are looking back on it, so it is very easy for us to distinguish these things. But before the cross, God's people had to learn of Christ's sacrifice by the object lesson God gave them, and it was a beautiful thing.

The cleansing of the sanctuary took place once a year, when the high priest went into the Most Holy Place. He had little bells on the hem of his robe, so the people outside would know that he was alive. If he went in there without first having cleansed his own sin, he would die. According to Jewish tradition, a cord was tied around him so that he could be pulled out if that were to happen. It was a solemn day.

The Day of Atonement was a specific day, and God has also set a specific day—the day to which the long-ago Day of Atonement pointed—for the beginning of the judgment of the entire world. Remember, the angel said to Daniel: "unto two thousand, three hundred days."

The Bible tells us that in prophecy a day stands for a year. One day equals one year; one week equals seven years. "And when you have completed them, lie again on your right side; then you shall bear the iniquity of the house of Judah forty days. I have laid on you a day for each year" (Ezekiel 4:6). "According to the number of the days in which you spied out the land, forty days, for each day you shall bear your guilt one year, namely forty years, and you shall know My rejection" (Numbers 14:34).

Remember that they searched the land for forty years, so this was a day/year principle being pointed out in Scripture. Every time that a day is mentioned in the Bible, of course, it doesn't necessarily mean a year, but with Bible prophecy, you can know that this is true. So 2,300 days equals 2,300 years.

So when does the 2,300-year prophecy in Daniel 8 begin? The Bible tells us that it begins with a specific command. In Daniel the ninth chapter, verses 22 and 23, we read:

"And he informed me, and talked with me, and said, 'O Daniel, I have now come forth to give you skill to understand. At the beginning of your supplications the command went out, and I have come to tell you, for you are greatly beloved; therefore consider the matter, and understand the vision.'"

With the angel's help, Daniel understood his visions. "Know therefore and understand, that from the going forth of the command to restore and build Jerusalem" (Daniel 9:25).

So this is our starting point for this 2,300-year prophecy—a certain command that goes forth. We know from history that the command "to restore and build Jerusalem" went forth in the seventh year of the reign of Artaxerxes, in 457 B.C. He had given several decrees, but this is the one that was acted upon. He gave the decree that they should go and rebuild Jerusalem and that anyone who wanted to go back to Jerusalem could go back. What a fantastic decree this was for the Hebrews.

Another prophecy began at exactly the same time as the 2,300-year prophecy—a prophecy of 70 weeks. "Seventy weeks are determined for your people and for your holy city" (Daniel 9:24). The word *determined* used here means "cut off."

So we cut off 70 weeks from that 2,300-year prophecy. Seventy weeks, times seven days, would be 490 days—or 490 years. So 490 years is cut off from that longer 2,300-year prophecy.

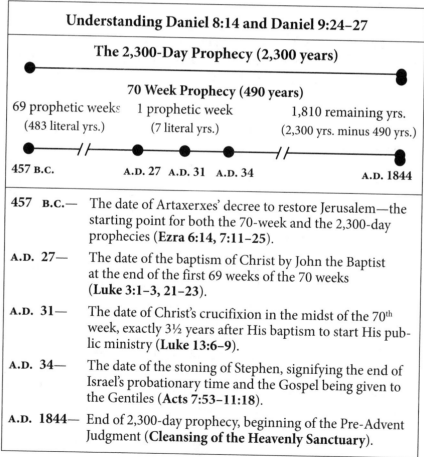

Understanding Daniel 8:14 and Daniel 9:24–27

The 2,300-Day Prophecy (2,300 years)

70 Week Prophecy (490 years)

69 prophetic weeks (483 literal yrs.)	1 prophetic week (7 literal yrs.)	1,810 remaining yrs. (2,300 yrs. minus 490 yrs.)

457 B.C. A.D. 27 A.D. 31 A.D. 34 A.D. 1844

457 B.C.— The date of Artaxerxes' decree to restore Jerusalem—the starting point for both the 70-week and the 2,300-day prophecies (**Ezra 6:14, 7:11–25**).

A.D. 27— The date of the baptism of Christ by John the Baptist at the end of the first 69 weeks of the 70 weeks (**Luke 3:1–3, 21–23**).

A.D. 31— The date of Christ's crucifixion in the midst of the 70th week, exactly 3½ years after His baptism to start His public ministry (**Luke 13:6–9**).

A.D. 34— The date of the stoning of Stephen, signifying the end of Israel's probationary time and the Gospel being given to the Gentiles (**Acts 7:53–11:18**).

A.D. 1844— End of 2,300-day prophecy, beginning of the Pre-Advent Judgment (**Cleansing of the Heavenly Sanctuary**).

At this point, the Bible says that after 69 of the 70 weeks, something would happen.

> "Know therefore and understand, that from the going forth of the command to restore and build Jerusalem until Messiah the Prince, there shall be seven weeks and sixty-two weeks [7 + 62 = 69]; the street shall be built again, and the wall, even in troublesome times." (Daniel 9:25)

This command to rebuild Jerusalem starts with the decree of Artaxerxes, and it takes us through time to the Messiah the Prince. The Jewish people do not accept the book of Daniel. They don't accept it because it is so precise. If they were to accept the book of Daniel, they would have to accept Jesus Christ because there is no one else who fits into the prophecy at the end of that 490-year period except Jesus.

Anyone else—all imposters and false christs—have long since fallen by the wayside. There has been no indication of anyone ever putting any kind of stamp of approval upon their ministry, but when Christ was baptized, the heavens opened, and these words came down: "This is my beloved son, in whom I am well pleased" (Matthew 3:17). So if the Jewish people accepted the book of Daniel, they would not be able to exclude Jesus as the Messiah the Prince. How long was it to be? The timeline was to be seventy weeks, or 490 years.

If we simply extend the beginning point of both the 2,300 years and the 490 years—457 B.C.—down through time, we arrive at A.D. 27. What happened in A.D. 27? We know that Christ was baptized in A.D. 27. We don't just know it by adding together those days from 457 B.C.—we also know it from the Gospel of Luke:

> "Now in the fifteenth year of the reign of Tiberius Caesar, Pontius Pilate being governor of Judea, Herod being tetrarch of Galilee, his brother Philip tetrarch of Iturea and the region of Trachonitis, and Lysanias tetrarch of Abilene." (Luke 3:1)

History is clear that the fifteenth year of Tiberius Caesar was the year A.D. 27—the very year Christ was baptized and began His ministry. "The time is fulfilled, and the kingdom of God is at hand. Repent, and believe in the gospel" (Mark 1:15). The time was fulfilled.

Jesus was a man of time. He arrived on the scene at precisely the right time, and when He went down into that water and was baptized. He was baptized at exactly the time that Bible prophecy in the book of Daniel had said that He would in A.D. 27. It was a fulfillment of the prophecies of Daniel:

> "When He had been baptized, Jesus came up immediately from the water; and behold, the heavens were opened to Him, and He saw the Spirit of God descending like a dove and alighting upon Him. And suddenly a voice came from heaven, saying, "This is My beloved Son, in whom I am well pleased." (Matthew 3:16, 17)

Jesus was to confirm the covenant for one week, and in the midst of the week, He would cause the sacrifice and the offering to cease. For three-and-a-half years, Christ's ministry was focused entirely on the Jewish people.

> "Then he [Jesus] shall confirm a covenant with many for one week; but in the middle of the week He shall bring an end to sacrifice and offering. And on the wing of abominations shall be one who makes desolate, even until the consummation, which is determined, is poured out on the desolate." (Daniel 9:27)

You remember the Samarian woman who wanted Jesus to bless her, and Jesus replied, "I was not sent except to the lost sheep of the house of Israel." To this she responded, "Even the little dogs eat the crumbs which fall from the Master's table" (Matthew 15:24, 26).

That was Christ's ministry for three-and-a-half years, and then He went to the cross, "cut off," as Daniel 9:26 says, but not for Himself. He didn't die for Himself, for He was sinless. He died for you and me, and for another three-and-a-half years after being cut off in the midst, we see the gospel directed only to the Jews. Then, in A.D. 34, Stephen was stoned, and that ended the limited ministry directed specifically to the Jews. After that, the gospel went to the whole world—at the end of that one-week or seven-year period.

> "Not that He should offer Himself often, as the high priest enters the Most Holy Place every year with blood of another—He then would have had to suffer often since the foundation of the world; but now, once at the end of the ages, He has appeared to put away sin by the sacrifice of Himself." (Hebrews 9:25, 26)

Christ was the very Lamb of God, and His ministry, being cut off in the midst of the week, would cause the sacrifice and offering system to cease. Matthew chapter 27, and verse 51, tells about that curtain being split, which literally did cause the sacrifice to cease in the temple: "Then, behold, the veil of the temple was torn in two from top to bottom; and the earth quaked, and the rocks were split" (Matthew 27:51). "From top to bottom"—some say that the temple curtain was anywhere from fourteen to eighteen inches thick, built with different fabrics lined and sewn together. It was impossible for it to be rent, or torn, by the hand of man—it was rent by the hand of God. So this one week is the time of the ministry allotted specifically to the Jews, and it did come to an end.

What then happened to the rest of these 2,300 years? Adding the remaining 1,810 years after the 490 years takes us to A.D. 1844. Did anything happen in A.D. 1844? The Bible tells us very clearly that at the end of those 2,300 years, a judgment was to take place, and the sanctuary was to be cleansed.

We looked at the cleansing of the sanctuary—the Day of Atonement, a day of judgment. The Bible says that a judgment was to begin at the end of the 2,300 years.

Numerous people don't realize that the judgment that began in heaven at the end of the 2,300 years—beginning with those who lived first, Cain, Abel, and right down the line—will actually be over before Christ returns the second time to earth. You see, some have thought that the judgment is going to be after His second coming.

Yes, there *is* one phase of the judgment that we will see afterward, but the investigative judgment of the living and the dead takes place prior to Christ's return. We know this because it says so in Revelation 22:12: "Behold, I am coming quickly, and My reward *is* with Me, to give to every one according to his work."

How could the reward be with Him, if there has been no judgment? You see, by this time, all will have been judged. The judgment will be already set. The Bible tells us that it started at the end of the 2,300-year period in 1844, but who is the judge?

"For the Father judges no one, but has committed all judgment to the Son" (John 5:22). Here, the Bible says that Jesus Himself is the Judge. We've always had the view that God the Father stands up somewhere and that He is the Judge. But No! Scripture says that Christ is the Judge. If He's the Judge, you're going to get a pretty fair trial, aren't you? You certainly are, if you are covered by His blood. You don't have to worry about this judgment. You don't ever have to worry about anything that you have ever done coming up in that judgment; it simply won't come up if you're covered by the blood of Jesus Christ. Your name will come up, but Christ will say, "My blood covers him (or her)," and you are found innocent. Now, I like that kind of trial. Every one of us should make sure that the blood of Jesus is covering our sins.

Let's look further at this scene. "Then the temple of God was opened in heaven, and the ark of His covenant was seen in His temple. And there were lightnings, noises, thunderings, an earthquake, and great hail" (Revelation 11:19).

You see, the sanctuary on earth was a copy of the very sanctuary that is in heaven. The judgment taking place there now is similar to the way it took place here in Old Testament times. This gives us an indication of how and what is taking place within the portals of heaven at this very moment.

Notice the three great books that will be vitally important in the great judgment in heaven:

- **The Book of Life:** "I saw the dead, small and great, standing before God, and books were opened. And another book was opened, which is the Book of Life. And the dead were judged according to their works, by the things which were written in the books" (Revelation 20:12).

- **The Book of Remembrance:** "Then those who feared the Lord spoke to one another, and the Lord listened and heard them; so a book of remembrance was written before Him for those who fear the Lord and who meditate on His name" (Malachi 3:16).

- **The Book of Iniquity:** "'For though you wash yourself with lye, and use much soap, yet your iniquity is marked before Me,' says the Lord God" (Jeremiah 2:22).

If you receive Jesus Christ, then your name is written in the book of life. You are saved or born again. If you do things that are good, those things are written in the book of remembrance, but those things won't save you, if your name isn't written in the book of life. If you do something that is bad, and all of us have, your name is written in the book of iniquity. The only way we keep that name in the book of life is to continue to accept Jesus and trust in Him day by day—that's the only way. There is not any other way we can be saved, except by the blood of Jesus. You can't do it on your own.

"For whoever shall keep the whole law, and yet stumble in one point, he is guilty of all" (James 2:10). Whenever we have sinned at any time, our names are written in the book of iniquity, and we can't be saved without the blood of Jesus. Each of us has to have the blood of Jesus to cover our sins because whatever mistakes we've made, we are guilty of everything. Who hasn't made a mistake? The only ones who think that they haven't are the ones who make the biggest mistake when they say or think that they haven't sinned in the sight of God.

Many people come to the place where they have "sanctification by senility." They become so decrepit in their bodies that they don't have any desire to sin anymore. Do you know what I mean? It is all taken away. If we had our health back, and we had all of the old blood running through us as it used to, we'd be just as sinful as we were. That is sanctification by senility.

So you see, we can only have sanctification by the blood of Jesus covering us. As Christ takes full control of us, that's the only true victory that comes in the life of the believer.

"Most assuredly, I say to you, he who hears My word and believes in Him who sent Me has everlasting life, and shall not come into judgment, but has passed from death into life" (John 5:24). The words of Jesus Christ assure us that if we believe on Him, we have passed from death unto life, and we don't have to be afraid of the great white throne judgment because we have accepted Him.

"Therefore He is also able to save to the uttermost those who come to God through Him, since He always lives to make intercession for them" (Hebrews 7:25). Our Intercessor, Jesus, is standing before God.

"If we confess our sins, He is faithful and just to forgive us our sins and to cleanse us from all unrighteousness" (1 John 1:9). If you confess your sins and trust in Jesus Christ, He will plead His blood for you. My friend, if you have done that, your sanctuary is cleansed. Jesus cleanses you of all sin, and you trust in Him for eternal life.

One of these days, it is going to all be over. Sometimes, we "play church," you might say, and we may think, "Well, maybe I can come along and kind of be a part of this—but not really."

God says, "You've got to become part of Me." You've got to become part of Jesus Christ because one of these days that judgment going on in heaven is going to be over, and at that time it will be too late to make a decision. At that time, Jesus the Judge will say, "He who is unjust, let him be unjust still; he who is filthy, let him be filthy still; he who is righteous, let him be righteous still; he who is holy, let him be holy still" (Revelation 22:11).

Christ can no longer do anything for you after that. Now is the time when He can. Now is the day of salvation.

A young man came into town one day with a team of horses. As he was coming into town, the horses got away. They began to run and got that old bridle in their teeth. The young man knew that down at the end of that street, the road turned sharply, then led to a large drop-off down a river bank. He knew that if he went off there, there was no way he could survive.

His horses had been frightened by a couple of dogs that had been chasing each other, and the young man was now doing everything he could to stop those horses, but he couldn't.

Suddenly, a long, lean fellow came from somewhere off to the side and jumped in to grab the bridle of one horse, then the ear of the other, which he twisted. Finally, he got the horses stopped and saved the young man's life.

A few weeks later, the young man was back in town again, and this time drank too much and got into a fight in the local bar. He pulled a gun and shot an innocent man and killed him.

They took him to jail. In those days, judgment was swift, so they soon took him to trial. When he walked into the courtroom, he saw, dressed in a judge's robe, the man who had earlier saved his life. The young man almost broke into a run toward that judge.

"Judge, judge," he cried out, "save me! You saved my life before—save me now." The judge replied, "The other day, I was your savior, but now I'm your judge."

Right now, Jesus is your Savior. If you accept Him, then when you stand as your name comes up in the judgment, Jesus pleads His blood for you—you don't have a thing to worry about. My friend, if you are tempted to put off accepting Him, don't do it. It's dangerous! One day, He will be your Judge, and without His blood covering your sins, you don't have a chance.

CHAPTER 3

What Is Going on in Heaven Right Now?

Daniel Webster once was asked at a public meeting what was the greatest thought that ever crossed his mind. His earnest, thoughtful reply was: "My personal accountability to God."

When I was a young boy, a statement my father sometimes used made a great impression upon me. When I was feeling especially lazy (and that was often), I would say to my father, "Well, do I *have* to do this?"

I can never forget his answer. "No, you don't have to do anything but die."

Death is a reality and something that can be avoided only for a while, for the Bible says, "It is appointed for men to die once, but after this the judgment" (Hebrews 9:27).

Judgment is something none of us can escape because God has summoned the entire world to appear in the judgment. Follow closely as I share the summons: "For we must all appear before the judgment seat of Christ, that each one may receive the things done in the body, according to what he has done, whether good or bad" (2 Corinthians 5:10).

No mistake is found here. Don't think for a minute you can break this appointment—"For we must *all* appear before the judgment seat of Christ."

Lenin, Stalin, Hitler, Mussolini, hypocrites, atheists—all people both good and bad—will appear in this judgment. Ministers of churches will appear, along with their congregations. Judges of courts, officers of the law, inmates of prisons, men and women, boys and girls, the sick and the healthy—all will have to respond to this high court summons. Yes, "we must *all* appear before the judgment seat of Christ." Every thought, every word, and every action of the whole life will be brought into review. In this judgment there will be no bribing of the jury or fixing of the case with the judge. There will be no loopholes in the law.

A skeptic wrote his county newspaper and said, "I planted, cultivated, and dug my potatoes on the Sabbath day, and this was the biggest yield I ever had." He continued, "Please explain to me the text that says, 'God rewards the good and punishes the bad.'"

An old grandmother read the article and wrote this to the editor: "Tell your infidel friend that God doesn't make full settlement in October."

The Bible says, "Because the sentence against an evil work is not executed speedily, therefore the heart of the sons of men is fully set in them to do evil" (Ecclesiastes 8:11).

While men have been making history, God has been keeping records in the books of heaven. Remember the portrait of the judgment, as we first noted it in the previous chapter:

"I watched till thrones were put in place, and the Ancient of Days was seated; His garment was white as snow, and the hair of His head was like pure wool. His throne was a fiery flame, its wheels a burning fire; a fiery stream issued and came forth from before Him. A thousand thousands ministered to Him; ten thousand times ten thousand stood before Him. The court was seated, and the books were opened." (Daniel 7:9, 10)

The Bible says we will be personally responsible for our own choices in the judgment: "But every one shall die for his own iniquity" (Jeremiah 31:30). "So then each of us shall give account of himself to God" (Romans 14:12).

In the judgment, God's divine law will be the standard, or norm. "So speak and so do as those who will be judged by the law of liberty" (James 2:12). I'm thankful that the standard in the judgment is a law of liberty.

To understand what God means when He speaks of the law as a law of liberty, you must first have it written in your heart by the miracle of the "new birth." Obeying God's commandments is not something we *have* to do; rather, it is a service of love that makes one free indeed in Christ Jesus. God's law for the Christian is a law of liberty—a law that drives the sinner to Christ for forgiveness and liberty.

It should be understood that liberty does not mean liberty to sin. Paul said, "Do we then make void the law through faith? Certainly not! On the contrary, we establish the law" (Romans 3:31).

The Bible teaches that the purpose of God's law is to reveal sin: "For by the law is the knowledge of sin" (Romans 3:20). It also instructs that "whosoever committeth sin transgresseth also the law: for sin is the transgression of the law" (1 John 3:4 KJV).

If God's law no longer existed, then sin would no longer exist. It would be no more than someone's interpretation. Defining sin would rest in man's hands instead of in God's. It is indeed a strange phenomenon, when an attempt is made to prove that the Ten Commandments have been destroyed. Whether we believe in God's commandments or not, they will be the standard in the judgment.

All of your sins and mine are recorded in the books of heaven. We cannot change one iota of our record. Nevertheless, our record need not condemn us. By repentance and perfect surrender, we can turn our case over to Jesus, who will write at the bottom of the ugly list, "I, even I, am He who blots out your transgressions for My own sake; and I will not remember your sins" (Isaiah 43:25).

If you are not ready to face the judgment, why not make plans today? The Bible teaches that only those clothed with Christ's righteousness will pass through the judgment. Our "righteousnesses are like filthy rags" (Isaiah 64:6).

We cannot change this condition, any more than the Ethiopian can change his skin or the leopard his spots (Jeremiah 13:23). But, thank God, provision for cleansing has been made by Jesus Christ our Lord.

> "I will greatly rejoice in the Lord, my soul shall be joyful in my God; for He has clothed me with the garments of salvation, He has covered me with the robe of righteousness, as a bridegroom decks himself with ornaments, and as a bride adorns herself with her jewels." (Isaiah 61:10)

Entrance into the kingdom of heaven will not be ours because of our goodness or our righteousness but because we have accepted Christ as our Lord and Savior and are clothed with His righteousness.

When the realization breaks on us that we are judgment bound and must stand in the Supreme Court of heaven, the question always comes, "When will it take place?" The Bible answers this for us. In Acts 24:25, we read the account of the apostle Paul as he stood in the presence of Felix: "Now as he reasoned about righteousness, self-control, and the judgment to come, Felix was afraid and answered, 'Go away for now; when I have a convenient time I will call for you.'"

We learn here that Paul was well aware of the fact that the judgment was future in his day. Next, let's review what the first angel said about the judgment in Revelation 14:6, 7:

> "Then I saw another angel flying in the midst of heaven, having the everlasting gospel to preach to those who dwell on the earth—to every nation, tribe, tongue, and people—saying with a loud voice, 'Fear God and give glory to Him, for the hour of His judgment has

come; and worship Him who made heaven and earth, the sea and springs of water.'"

This angel's message became a reality in being proclaimed to the world at the end of the 2,300-year prophecy of Daniel 8:14, which began with the decree in 457 B.C. to restore Jerusalem and was consummated in the year 1844. When we compare scripture with scripture, we find that at the end of the 2,300 days the sanctuary of heaven was to be cleansed. This constituted the beginning of the investigative judgment.

So the judgment, which was future in Paul's day, actually began in heaven in 1844—the same time that the message of Revelation 14:6, 7 began to be heralded to all the world. For more than a century the investigative judgment has been in progress. Truly, this is a sobering thought.

This judgment is currently reviewing the names of all who have ever confessed God's name. The first name called in this judgment was Abel, for he was the first man to die on this earth. One by one, the names continue to be reviewed—first of the dead and then of the living. None of us can be sure when our name will be reviewed, but we do know that this judgment precedes the return of Christ in order to make ready for His coming.

Some day soon, your name and mine will be called. We will be judged by the law of God. Unless we claim Christ as our personal Savior, confessing our sins to Him, our names will be blotted out. This very thing is alluded to in Revelation 22:11, 12:

"He who is unjust, let him be unjust still; he who is filthy, let him be filthy still; he who is righteous, let him be righteous still; he who is holy, let him be holy still. And behold, I am coming quickly, and My reward *is* with Me, to give to every one according to his work."

If your name were called right now, how would it be with you?

In an old-fashioned village in Germany stands a cathedral that is no longer used as a house of worship, but now serves as a museum. On the wall is a picture that represents the judgment. Christ is seated on His throne. Just in front of Christ is a great concourse of people as far as the eye can see. Standing in front of the people is an angel, holding in his hand a pair of balances. Over the balances, a hand has written: "Weighed in the Balances and Found Wanting."

The hand seems to be waiting for the answer—"worthy" or "wanting." When our lives are weighed in the great balances of heaven, dear friend, what will it be? Your decision for or against Christ will decide the outcome.

CHAPTER 4

The ~~Nine~~ Ten Commandments

Czar Nicholas of Russia was walking one day through the royal gardens. Suddenly, he came to a stop. Right in the middle of the garden a guard was standing at attention. The czar looked around to see what he was guarding. He could see nothing in the garden to be protected, so he stepped up to him and asked, "Why are you stationed in this garden? What are you guarding?"

"I am stationed here because I was so ordered by the sergeant of the guard. There is always a guard here—twenty-four hours of the day."

The czar turned and said, "I want to see the sergeant of the guard."

When the sergeant arrived, he asked, "Sergeant, why is this guard standing here in this specific spot, and why is a guard always standing here?"

"I do not know," the sergeant replied. "The captain of the guard gave me the order. We have always had a guard there ever since I can remember."

So the czar said, "Summon the captain." The captain came, and when asked why the guard was placed there in the garden, he replied that it was because the order was written in the book. So they sent for the book, and it was written there very clearly that a guard was to occupy that spot in the garden.

Why? Because some 200 years earlier when Catherine the Great had planted a rose bush in that garden, she had also placed a guard there to prevent anyone from trampling the bush. The rose bush had long since died, but there had always been a guard right there because no one had stopped and dared to ask why.

You laugh and say that such a thing could not happen today. But do you know that today people are standing guard over some teachings—some doctrines—that are just as dead as Catherine's rose bush as far as the Bible is concerned? Absolutely, positively, not to be found in the Bible are some things that men today hold very sacred.

People frequently ask me why I keep Saturday as the Sabbath. First, I would like to tell you that I and others in my church do not keep Saturday as the Sabbath just to be different. It does make us different, in spite of ourselves, but this is not the reason we keep it. We keep the Sabbath for the same reason that most Christians refrain from stealing, from committing adultery, from lying, and from coveting.

Friends, we are saved only through the grace of the Lord Jesus Christ—through His blood. I have never found anyone in the world who would think of accusing a moral man of being a legalist because he was honest. I have never found anyone accusing the missionary of a Sunday-keeping group of being a legalist because it teaches the heathen not to bow down in front of idols. Yet, when you find someone teaching a specific commandment—one of God's commands—then people throw up their hands and say, "Oh, you're a legalist. This commandment is different from the other ten."

But is it? We find that a lot of honest people have wondered about the seventh-day Sabbath, since it is very clearly taught in the Ten Commandments. We find that they have a lot of questions about this subject. They want to know why the majority of Christians today go to church on a day that is different from the one the Bible directs us to keep. They want to know when this day was changed, for obviously there has been a change in the day of worship.

Before going any further in this discussion, I want to read a text found in 1 Corinthians 2:1, 2:

"And I, brethren, when I came to you, did not come with excellence of speech or of wisdom declaring to you the testimony of God. For I determined not to know anything among you except Jesus Christ and Him crucified."

Paul put the emphasis right where it should be—on Christ. As we study this subject, I too want the emphasis to be on Christ our Lord and Savior. The Bible says that the Lord has a particular day. We often hear the expression "The Lord's Day." Actually, it is found in only one place in the Bible—in Revelation 1:10: "I was in the Spirit on the Lord's Day."

All that this text tells us is that the Lord has a day. It doesn't say which day it is. It does not say if it is Sunday, Monday, Tuesday, Wednesday, Thursday, or Friday. It says absolutely nothing about that. It simply says that the Lord has a day. If this is correct, then I think we must find other texts and see what they can tell us about this day. Now, someone asks, "Are you going through the Bible looking up these texts?" Yes, that is exactly what we are going to do.

Let us say that I put a pole in my yard and ask you to sight along that pole in a straight line. Now, what you would see would depend entirely on where you stand. Someone else sighting along that pole from a different place would say that it points in a different direction.

This is one of the problems in Christianity today. People take isolated texts and read into them their own preconceived ideas. They take a very shallow look at what they read. But if you will take all the texts of Scripture on one subject and piece them together, then you will see an entirely different story. You will see what God wants you to know.

In Matthew 12:8 we find a text concerning the Lord's Day: "For the Son of Man is Lord even of the Sabbath."

If that text had said that Jesus was Lord of the first day, I would not argue with the text because Christ is the one who said it. Again, in the Bible we find Jesus making reference to the Sabbath and speaking of Himself as being the Lord of that day: "He said to them, 'The Sabbath was made for man, and not man for the Sabbath. Therefore the Son of Man is also Lord of the Sabbath'" (Mark 2:27, 28).

These verses truly leave no room for doubt. The Lord's Day is the seventh-day Sabbath. In the Old Testament, too, God gives information as to which day is His:

"Thus the heavens and the earth, and all the host of them, were finished. And on the seventh day God ended His work which He had done, and He rested on the seventh day from all His work which He had done. Then God blessed the seventh day and sanctified it, because in it He rested from all His work which God had created and made." (Genesis 2:1-3)

Someone might say, "I just do not see what difference it makes. I just do not see that Saturday is any different from any other day." But Christ made the difference right back there at the time of Creation. He made the difference. Six days were all the same, one right after another, and then came the seventh day. The Bible tells us that He blessed it, and He sanctified it. Now the word "sanctify" means to set aside as holy. The seventh day is sanctified—set aside—for a holy purpose.

Just why is Jesus Lord of the Sabbath day? He is Lord of the Sabbath day not only because He set it aside for a holy purpose but also because He created it. The One who created this world and brought everything into existence brought the seventh-day Sabbath into existence as part of the Creation:

> "For by Him all things were created that are in heaven and that are on earth, visible and invisible, whether thrones or dominions or principalities or powers. All things were created through Him and for Him." (Colossians 1:16)

Notice too, Hebrews 1:1, 2: "God … has in these last days spoken to us by His Son, whom He has appointed heir of all things, through whom also He made the worlds."

No wonder Jesus said that He was Lord of the Sabbath. He was Lord of the Sabbath because He had created the Sabbath. He made it at the time of Creation. Note with me these verses:

- "In the beginning God created the heavens and the earth" (Genesis 1:1).

- "Then God blessed the seventh day and sanctified it" (Genesis 2:3).

- "All things were made through Him, and without Him nothing was made that was made" (John 1:3).

This is why Jesus honored the Sabbath, and this is the reason His followers today continue to honor that which Christ set as an example. Some people say, "I have always understood that the Sabbath was made for the Jews." But we have just read in Genesis that the Sabbath was instituted at the time of Creation.

Let me ask you something. This world was created and given to Adam. All of the animals, plants, and everything else on earth was given to him, and the Sabbath was given to Adam at the same time. What nationality was Adam? Was Adam a Jew? Was he Irish? Was Adam Italian? Or French? What was he? Adam was just a man, wasn't he? He was simply the father of mankind—no particular nationality at all.

So everything that God created and gave to Adam, He gave to all mankind. For instance, God gave to Adam a woman. He gave Eve to Adam. If it is true that the Sabbath was only for the Jews, then it would also have to be true that women were created only for the Jews. Yet, a woman was given as a companion to Adam just as the Sabbath was given. Clearly, God created the Sabbath and gave it to all mankind.

Let us suppose that the following conversation took place just after Creation. I'm sure it didn't, but just in our imagination, let's pretend that the angel Gabriel is walking around with the Creator, looking at everything.

"Oh, this is beautiful," Gabriel says. "You've done such a wonderful job here. All these things that You have created are wonderful, but there is one thing that bothers me."

"What is that, Gabriel?"

"It is the Sabbath—why did You create the Sabbath?"

"The Sabbath is for the Jews," the Creator replies.

"But there aren't any Jews."

"That's all right," the Creator says, "but they will be around—they'll be here."

So they sit down for two thousand years—104,000 Sabbaths—waiting for the first Jew to come along to keep the Sabbath. Do you think that was the way it happened? Hardly! That which was created at Creation was given to mankind and was meant for all men. The Sabbath was a part of this world even before sin existed.

Sometimes people get all the different laws mixed up. As we have studied this word, *Sabbath*, we have seen that the Ten Commandments and the ceremonial laws are two separate and distinct laws. One was written on tables of stone by the finger of God and placed inside the ark of the covenant in the Most Holy Place. The other was written on parchments by the hand of Moses and placed beside the ark. One expresses the everlasting principle of righteousness, the character of God, the Ten Commandments. The other was a set of laws given because sin had come in—laws given only to point forward to the coming and death of Jesus Christ on the cross; laws soon to be completely done away with because they were no longer necessary. These temporary laws pointed to the Lamb of God, and when the Lamb of God came, this, of course, made these laws no longer necessary.

Some people try to take the fourth commandment out of the middle of the Ten Commandments and place it with the ceremonial laws. Some say, "I'll go along with nine of the ten. I agree it is wrong to bow down before other gods, to steal, and to commit adultery, but there is one thing there that should not be there, and if you will take the fourth commandment out and replace it, then everything will be all right."

But God is the one who placed the fourth as one of the ten, so who am I to remove it? This fourth commandment was given before sin ever even came in—and for a very important reason.

Someone else says, "Yes, but now listen. The Sabbath was never kept before Sinai." Well, that simply isn't true. The Sabbath *was* kept before Sinai. The Bible even tells us that Abraham kept the commandments: "Abraham obeyed My voice and kept My charge, My commandments, My statutes, and My laws" (Genesis 26:5).

Joseph too kept the commandments when he was fleeing from Potiphar's wife. He said, "How can I do this great wickedness and sin against God?" (Genesis 39:9). People sometimes forget that the precepts of the Decalogue—the principles of righteousness—are everlasting. In fact, the children of Israel even kept the Ten Commandments, including the Sabbath commandment, before the commandments were given at Mt. Sinai. This is found in Exodus 16. Look it up and read it sometime.

The manna was given to them in a double portion on Friday, and no manna fell on Sabbath. So they were keeping the Sabbath even before Sinai. By the way, when the commandments were given to them, this was not the first time that the commandments had been given by any means.

God had shown to man the plan of salvation in the Garden of Eden and repeated it to Abraham. Man had been clearly made to know what was right and what was wrong, and it had been passed from generation to generation. But after the people of God had been taken into the land of Egypt, the land of bondage, they mixed with the sons of men until they became degraded, and it was necessary for God to give the law again by special revelation. That's the reason it was given on Mt. Sinai.

Another might add, "I know that the seventh day is the Sabbath in the Bible, but we keep the first day in honor of the resurrection because He rose from the grave on that day."

I would like to say that there is absolutely no doubt that the first day of the week is the day of the resurrection. However, I would like to ask a question. By what authority do men keep it as a holy day? You can search the Scriptures from cover to cover, and neither in the Old or the New Testament can you find any command to keep the first day of the week holy. There is no place in the Bible where you can find that the seventh-day Sabbath has been done away with as the day of worship.

Now, back to the resurrection—two very important things happened on that weekend. On Friday was the crucifixion—on Sunday was the resurrection. Now, one is just as important as the other. Without the crucifixion, there could be no resurrection. So if we follow the idea of keeping Sunday, the first day of the week, because of the resurrection, it would be just as good to say that we should keep Friday in honor of the crucifixion. But we are not given the right—we are not given the authority anywhere in God's Word—to set up or designate a day for worship. This is something that God Himself did. God is the one we worship, and if we are going to worship God, why not at least respect His right to tell us on what day we should worship, instead of trying to pick some other day we'd prefer to worship Him?

Sometimes I hear people say that it just doesn't make any difference. Remember those two important events that happened: the crucifixion and the resurrection. It seems as if God would give us something to commemorate these two events—and He did. In 1 Corinthians 11:20, we read of the communion service—one of the ordinances given to Christ's church.

By the way, in the Old Testament were all sorts of ceremonies and ordinances, but in the New Testament, only two ordinances were given. However, the devil has diluted them until neither one has much meaning in the minds of individuals today. Yet in 1 Corinthians 11:26 we read: "For as often as you eat this bread and drink this cup, you proclaim the Lord's death till He comes."

So the communion service was to commemorate the crucifixion of Christ. Every time you take the communion bread, and every time you drink the wine, you are commemorating the death of our Lord and Savior, Jesus Christ.

Then again, in the New Testament we read: "Therefore we were buried with Him through baptism into death, that just as Christ was raised from the dead by the glory of the Father, even so we also should walk in newness of life" (Romans 6:4).

Yes, Christ did give something to commemorate the resurrection. That glorious day when Christ came forth—the Redeemer of the world, the Victor over death—He came forward to give us eternal life. Baptism represents His death, His burial, and His resurrection. Bible baptism is a beautiful ordinance, but man has changed it. Man has taken away the beauty and meaning of baptism. Later on, we are going to look at baptism and how man has changed it. Will God honor man's change?

Some will say, "If what you say is true, do we know for sure what day the Sabbath is? Has the calendar been changed?"

I would also like to say that the Jewish people have their calendar. It is something like 4,000 years old and has been followed without interruption down through the years. Now, their dates differ a little bit from ours, but there is one thing that does not differ—and that is the weekly cycle.

Now, there has been one change in our calendar, the Julian calendar, since the time of Christ. The Julian calendar had 365 days in a year. But how many are there precisely? That's right—365¼. This calendar, however, did not allow for that one-fourth of a day. So as time went on, the calendar, as you can see, gradually fell out of step with the actual annual solar cycle.

But remember, the *weekly cycle* never changed. In the winter, when they were supposed to be having cold weather, they were having spring. So they realized that to get everything back in order, they had to make a change. A change took place in the year 1582, and to make the correction, they had to take ten days from the calendar.

Here is how they did it: Wednesday was October 3, Thursday was October 4, and—watch this now—Friday was October 15. Instead of Friday being October 5, they made it October 15. Saturday was October 16. So you see that you can change the numbers of the calendar all you want to, but you really haven't changed the calendar until you start fooling around with the days—the weekly cycle.

They had Wednesday coming just before Thursday, and Friday coming just after Thursday, and Saturday coming after Friday. So you see, the weekly cycle was not changed at all. One city in the world, Singapore, has twenty-seven different calendars in the area. Some are Chinese calendars, some are Jewish, some are Muslim—all kinds of calendars. They all disagree on everything—literally everything—except one thing, and that is the *weekly cycle*.

Astronomers tell us that as far as they can tell from the study of the stars, there has never been any time lost. You don't really have to go all the way back to the beginning of time—you only need to go back to the time of Christ. If there was anything wrong with the seventh-day Sabbath, He would have straightened people out then. He *did* straighten some of them out on the *way* they were keeping it. If it had been a different day, He would have told them at that time.

We still have Jewish calendars that date back to before the time of Christ, and there has been no change in the weekly cycle. It is sort of revealing to me that Catholics know when Sunday comes, Muslims know when Friday comes, but when a group of people say that they are going to follow the Bible Sabbath, they throw up their hands and say, "Oh, those poor people—they don't even know what day the Sabbath is." Yet, these same people have no trouble at all finding which day is Easter Sunday.

Friends, we have no trouble finding the seventh-day Sabbath of the Bible. The Bible tells us plainly that Christ was crucified on Friday, the preparation day. Then the Sabbath day drew on. The women went to their homes and prepared spices, but they did not take the spices to the grave because the Sabbath was drawing nigh. They rested the Sabbath, according to the commandment, and then on the first day of the week, they went to take the spices to Christ's tomb. They did not go there to worship—they went because they thought that Christ was dead. But when they got there, they found that He had risen. It speaks nowhere in the Scriptures of this being set aside as a day of worship. So actually, as a holy day, Sunday is purely manmade.

God says that the Sabbath should begin at sunset on the day of preparation and end at sunset on the Sabbath—the seventh day. But the majority of those who worship on Sunday keep the day from midnight till midnight. This comes from the decree of the pope saying that this is the way it is to be kept. When we are keeping a day from midnight till midnight, it can be changed very easily by the legislature. Twice a year, we go to daylight savings time and then back to standard time. When we do, those who worship from midnight to midnight have their day of worship changed immediately by one hour. But God set His timetable in the sky, and no one can change that. No matter if the hours are changed, God says that the Sabbath is to be kept from sunset till sunset.

You might ask, "What difference does it make, anyway?" "Does it really make any difference?"

Remember the story, in Genesis 4, of Cain and Abel and their sacrifices. Cain said, "It doesn't make any difference, and I'm not going to bring a blood sacrifice. I am going to bring the things that I grow. I am going to bring them myself. After all, it's in the spirit—if I've got the right spirit, then it's all right."

So Cain went to the fields and brought the things he had grown. He placed them on the altar and expected God to rain down fire—show His approval of his offering. Cain said he was sincere and honest, but he found that God would not honor his sacrifice because He had said that it was to be a blood sacrifice. Man says that it doesn't really make any difference on which day we worship.

This whole idea of it not making any difference is coming into our society on every level. We look at all of God's commandments. We look at the first one about worshiping other gods. Well, it really doesn't make any difference, some say, but if we start saying this about the first commandment, then we will also say it about the other commandments.

This is the reason today that we find immorality on the rampage. Today, we find people who read the commandment that says we should not commit adultery, and they say it really does not make any difference, just so long as there is "meaning" between two people.

Much of this state of things is the fault of preachers in the pulpit. If they had been saying, "Go back to the Bible—go back to the commandments of God and follow them," we would likely not have this complete moral breakdown. It is the responsibility of the church to uphold the commandments of God.

But instead of teaching men and women to live in harmony with God's commandments, we find that often, the church itself has led in changing or even doing away with the commandments that God said we should honor. "If you love Me, keep My commandments," Jesus said (John 14:15).

What does the Bible say about Sunday? I have heard, as some tell me, that there is a text that commands Sunday observance. Where is it? In the next chapter we will look at how the change of the day of worship came into the church and see if it is legitimate.

42

CHAPTER 5

Clearing the Fog about Day Number Seven

Some things are simple and clear. For example:

- ALWAYS RIGHT: To study about Jesus.
- NEVER WRONG: To follow His example.

But sometimes people—or even churches—make complicated and foggy those things that Jesus made simple and clear. One of those things that some have covered with fog is the plain teaching of the Bible about the seventh-day Sabbath.

When it comes to this or any other Bible truth, our only safety is to follow the example of Jesus. "For to this you were called, because Christ also suffered for us, leaving us an example, that you should follow His steps" (1 Peter 2:21).

Here are the Christian's marching orders. Here is the gospel commission to the individual Christian. Before we can *go*—which is what Jesus told us to do—we must first *come* and become like Him. In all things—in my habits, in practices, thoughts, actions, and words—I want to be like Jesus.

We discovered in the previous chapter that Christ's example, from the beginning to the end of His ministry, was a Sabbath-keeping example. As we might have walked down the street there in Nazareth on a Friday afternoon, we would have seen Jesus and his father Joseph scurrying about the carpenter shop, putting things in order, and then closing the door as the sun sank low in the west.

Let's quickly review what we've already explored, before we launch farther into this chapter. We discovered, way back there in the Garden of Eden, the Sabbath was given to the entire human race and not just to the Jews as part of Creation week. We noted that one of the three members of the Godhead was the active agent in Creation, and we discovered that the active Creator was Jesus Christ who—as He preexisted with the Father from the days of eternity—created this world. Then we read from the Ten Commandments and discovered that the very commandment that men forget is the one that God said to remember. We also learned who gave the Ten Commandments: "There is one Lawgiver, who is able to save" (James 4:12). "You shall call His name JESUS, for He will save His people from their sins" (Matthew 1:21).

The Ten Commandments, then, are Christian commandments, aren't they? So the question we face is this: With the counsel of Scripture so crystal clear that we could not misunderstand, why is it that we have two camps in the Christian world—one that believes that Christians ought to observe the first day of the week; the other that believes that the seventh day is the Sabbath of Christians, even in post-resurrection time? Who is right? How can we know?

As true followers of Jesus, we are not concerned with what any church teaches. We are only concerned about what the Word of God says.

> *What says the Bible, the blessed Bible?*
> *This may my only question be.*
> *Teachings of men so often mislead us;*
> *What says the Bible to me?*

That is our authority. That is the only place we can turn for help, for security, for a foundation for our faith. We must have a "thus saith the Lord," an "it is written," for every practice in our Christian experience.

The first day of the week as a day of worship has been quite widely accepted. But the question confronting us is, why? Surely, there must be a reason. Why is it that the majority of Christians admittedly observe a day other than the seventh day of the week, which we discussed?

If we are going to call ourselves Christians, then it goes without saying that we are going to take as authority for our belief the Word of God. If that is true, then it is only logical to conclude that we must find a Bible reason for setting aside a day so plainly spoken of in Scripture. So what we want to do in this chapter is to examine the basis upon which Sunday found its way into the Christian church, beginning with what the Bible has to say about the first day of the week.

We will not find the word *Sunday* there, since (with the exception of "the Sabbath" and "the preparation day") the Bible uses only numbers to designate the days of the week. We need to start back in the book of be-ginnings. We are going to see if we can discover the foundation on which Sunday observance rests. Here is our first pillar in the account of Creation week: "God called the light Day, and the darkness He called Night. So the evening and the morning were the first day" (Genesis 1:5).

It says nothing here about this first day being holy, sacred, or set aside as a day of worship. It says nothing about it, other than to list it as Creation's first day. Note one other important phrase in this verse: "the *evening and the morning* were the first day."

You see, the Bible day begins at evening, or at sunset. As we go on through Genesis 1, we discover that the evening and the morning were the second day, the third day, and so on. The Bible day begins at sunset. This is important for us to remember because we will refer to it again a little later. We haven't yet discovered anything here that would give us any sanction for the first day of the week as a day of worship—or any other day, for that matter.

Next, let's turn to some texts in the New Testament, concerning the life of our Lord that mention the first day of the week.

We have come to the experience of our Lord, and we must see what the New Testament tells us about the first day of the week. We must have a "thus saith the Lord" for this Christian practice if we're to follow it.

"Now after the Sabbath, as the first day of the week began to dawn, Mary Magdalene and the other Mary came to see the tomb" (Matthew 28:1).

You will recognize this immediately from the account of the crucifixion-resurrection weekend of our Lord. This is simply Matthew's account of the events that took place. Here again, this text does not tell us much, but notice that it says, "after the Sabbath, as the first day of the week began to dawn." It makes a distinction between the Sabbath and the first day of the week. This is the first mention of the first day of the week in the New Testament, but it does not give us much help. All right, let us go on.

We go next to the Gospel according to Mark. You will find these next few references are parallel accounts of this same crucifixion–resurrection weekend. "Now when the Sabbath was past, Mary Magdalene, Mary the mother of James, and Salome bought spices, that they might come and anoint Him. Very early in the morning, on the first day of the week, they came to the tomb when the sun had risen" (Mark 16:1, 2).

This verse does not tell us much about the day of worship—it's just a simple narration of the events. Notice a few verses later: "Now when He rose early on the first day of the week, He appeared first to Mary Magdalene, out of whom He had cast seven demons" (Mark 16:9).

Here again, just an historical account—nothing sets one day apart or above another but simply tells us that this was the day on which Jesus arose.

Now let's look at the next Gospel account in Luke: "That day was the Preparation, and the Sabbath drew near" (Luke 23:54).

We discovered the preparation was the day on which Jesus was cruci-fied—the sixth day of the week, or the day we commonly call Friday. The Christian world, of course, calls this day Good Friday.

> "The women who had come with Him from Galilee followed after, and they observed the tomb and how His body was laid. Then they returned and prepared spices and fragrant oils. And they rested on the Sabbath according to the commandment." (Luke 23:55, 56)

> "Now on the first day of the week, very early in the morning, they, and certain other women with them, came to the tomb bringing the spices which they had prepared." (Luke 24:1)

Again, in these two verses we find nothing about the first day of the week being sacred, and notice that the Sabbath is when Jesus was in the tomb. It would seem logical that if ever there were an excuse for the disciples to treat a bit lightly the seventh day of the week, they might have had an excuse here. Christ had been crucified. He was now in the tomb—His body needed to be prepared for burial. Apparently, though, they were still concerned about the Sabbath observance because as the Sabbath drew on, they returned to their homes and rested the Sabbath day, according to the commandment. We have discovered nothing here about the first day of the week being holy.

Now we go to John's account—the last of the Gospel narratives. "Now the first day of the week Mary Magdalene went to the tomb early, while it was still dark, and saw that the stone had been taken away from the tomb" (John 20:1). "Then, the same day at evening, being the first day of the week, when the doors were shut where the disciples were assembled, for fear of the Jews, Jesus came and stood in the midst, and said to them, 'Peace be with you'" (John 20:19).

Here we find a record of a first-day-of-the-week meeting in the New Testament after the resurrection of our Lord—no question about it. But I would like to ask you a question: "Were the disciples meeting here in honor of the resurrected Lord?" You respond, "Absolutely not! It says so right in that verse."

Were they meeting in honor of the resurrection? No, it doesn't say that. They were assembled "for fear of the Jews." Were they celebrating the resur-rection here? Absolutely not! Why, they didn't even believe that Christ had risen from the grave yet.

They were not setting aside a new day of worship, and they were not meeting in honor of the resurrection. They were not meeting in honor of anything. They were scared. That is what it says. Their Master had just been crucified, and they did not know but that, as His followers, the same fate might befall them. So they were meeting in the upper room, not in honor of the resurrection but "for fear of the Jews." They were talking over their plight: Where do we go from here? What happens now?

As we read on in this chapter, we notice that Jesus came and spoke to them and convinced them that He had risen from the grave—and they were startled. They thought they had seen a ghost because they had not yet believed that Jesus had risen from the grave. So we certainly cannot discover from this text anything having to do with Sunday sacredness or about anyone keeping a day holy.

We must find some record, surely, in the experience in the early church, and we do. "Now on the first day of the week, when the disciples came together to break bread, Paul, ready to depart the next day, spoke to them and continued his message until midnight" (Acts 20:7).

Ah, here it is—a meeting of the disciples on the first day of the week, but let me ask you several questions. Please carefully consider them because the answers are most important.

First of all, if we discovered that the disciples were meeting on the first day of the week, that they were celebrating the Lord's Supper, and that they were having a religious or preaching service, would that make that day holy? Second, does the meeting of Christian people on any day of the week set that day aside as day for Christians to worship? Finally, exactly what day of the week was it on which the disciples met here together?

Paul preached till midnight, remember? The Bible next says, "There were many lamps in the upper room where they were gathered together" (Acts 20:8).

Remember what we read back in Genesis 1: "The evening and the morning were the first day" (Genesis 1:5)—see the other days of Creation week too: verses 5, 8, 13, 19, 23, and 31. We discovered that the evening, in Bible reckoning, is the dark part of the day and comes first. Now let me ask you: "If this were the dark part of the first day of the week, it would be the time we now call Saturday night, would it not?" The New English Bible puts it this way: "On the Saturday night when we met in our assembly for the breaking of bread, Paul, who was to leave next day, addressed them, and went on speaking until midnight." So, you see, this isn't Seventh-day Adventist theology. This is just Bible reckoning. The dark part of the first day of the week would be what we call Saturday night.

The disciples met on Saturday night. They broke bread together. Now we have another thing to discover here. Does the breaking of bread make a day holy? Turn to Acts 2:46: "So continuing daily with one accord in the temple, and breaking bread from house to house, they [the disciples] ate their food with gladness and simplicity of heart."

Here is the record: They were breaking bread every day, and remember, Jesus gave them the communion service, the Lord's Supper, on what day of the week? It was what we now call Thursday night, the night before His crucifixion, which took place on Friday. Then, if we are going to say that when the disciples meet together to break bread, it makes the day holy, we are going to have to keep Thursday night. The point is simply this: Christian people meeting together to break bread does not make the day holy.

There is something else we ought to notice in Acts 20:7: "Now on the first day of the week, when the disciples came together to break bread [we learned that this was Saturday night], Paul, ready to depart the next day, spoke to them and continued his message until midnight."

From this story bear in mind that Eutychus, sitting in the window, fell asleep and fell from the window to his death. God miraculously brought the man to life again. Then Paul preached on through the rest of the night, it says, and the next morning—Sunday morning—he walked nineteen miles across the isthmus to Assos and caught a ship. This is now Sunday morning. So if Paul had a new belief, a new day to put in place of an old one that had been taken out of the way, he made a terrible mistake in doing this, didn't he?

The point, I think, is evident: Nothing in this text even suggests that the first day of the week was the day that had taken the place of the Sabbath that God had given to mankind. Of course not! Why should God change the day that was a token of His creative power? God was still the Creator—why should He change the memorial of that occasion? We discover from the pages of the New Testament that He did not.

Notice this text: "Now concerning the collection for the saints, as I have given orders to the churches of Galatia, so you must do also: On the first day of the week let each one of you lay something aside, storing up as he may prosper, that there be no collections when I come" (1 Corinthians 16:1, 2).

At first reading, someone may conclude it suggests here that we are to go to church and give an offering on the first day of the week. But is that really what the verse says? "On the first day of the week let each one of you lay something aside." Paul was making a missionary journey here, and they had endured an extended time of poverty and privation back in Jerusalem. So he sent a letter out and said: "If you will set aside some funds for the poor saints back in Jerusalem, I will pick it up. Do that the first of the week before you go out and start a new week of business. Then it will all be taken care of, and you won't have to do the bookkeeping after I get there."

That is what he is saying here. Nothing is even suggested here about a meeting. Nothing is suggested about going anywhere and giving an offering, not at all. We certainly have no evidence here on which to base a change of the day of worship from Saturday to Sunday.

God is not taken unaware by anything that happens. God knew a time of apostasy and falling away would come into the Christian church. As a matter of fact, the apostle Paul wrote about that. Some of the believers in Thessalonica believed that Christ was going to come within the next few months. The apostle wrote to them to assure them that there are some things that must take place before Jesus would come:

> "Let no one deceive you by any means; for that Day will not come unless the falling away comes first, and the man of sin is revealed, the son of perdition, who opposes and exalts himself above all that is called God or that is worshiped, so that he sits as God in the temple of God, showing himself that he is God." (2 Thessalonians 2:3, 4)

God said through the apostle Paul that a great apostasy would take place before Christ came back. Friends, scarcely were the bodies of the disciples cold in their graves before this apostasy began—"For the mystery of lawlessness is already at work" (2 Thessalonians 2:7)—already, compromise and apostasy were entering the early church.

During this time in sacred history, one after another of the apostles died, and other men rose to take their places. One after another of the great beliefs, the great teachings of Scripture, were compromised. During this time, for instance, baptism by immersion was replaced with baptism by sprinkling. Also, at this time prayers to God were replaced by prayers to the saints. We could go down the list of Christian truths and notice how, one after another, they were compromised.

This did not happen overnight. It took a period of generations, in some instances. However, it isn't difficult for us to see how that could happen because many have told us that their great concern is that the standards in their own churches are crumbling. It seems in just our own short lifetime virtually every Christian standard has been compromised and pushed aside by some churches in the interest of popularity. So it isn't hard for us to see how this compromise could come into the Christian church back in its earliest years, and that is exactly what happened.

The Sabbath was one of those compromised truths. Let me explain very briefly how it happened, and if you remember your history from this period, this will be familiar to you.

At the beginning of the Christian era, Sunday was popularly observed throughout the Roman world in public services during which hymns were chanted and prayers offered. As Christianity made its first impact on the people of that age, it was violently opposed by paganism. Scarcely had a century passed before semi-Christian philosophers were teaching in the church. Many of them taught that there was some good in all systems of religion and advocated the adoption of various pagan rites and practices.

For example, the peoples of the East had long been accustomed to worship with their faces toward the rising sun. Although this custom was vigorously condemned by Old Testament prophets (see Ezekiel 8:15, 16), the new teachers encouraged Christians also to face east in prayer "as the type of Christ the Sun of Righteousness."

Church leaders who desired to win pagans to Christianity endeavored to minimize the differences and multiply the points of resemblance between the two systems. Since Sunday was the day on which God began Creation and upon which Christ rose from the dead, ingenious teachers suggested that Christians might appropriately worship on the first day of the week. Over the course of decades, the fusion of the two philosophies became a reality.

Here is an interesting statement by Dr. Edward Hiscox, author of the *Baptist Church Manual*, from a paper before a Baptist ministers' conference in New York a number of years ago:

"There was and is a commandment to keep holy the Sabbath day, but that Sabbath day was not Sunday. It will be said, however, and with some show of triumph that the Sabbath was transferred from the seventh to the first day of the week, with all of its duties, privileges, and sanctions. Earnestly desiring information on this subject which I have studied for many years, I ask, where can the record of such a transaction be found? Not in the New Testament, absolutely not. There is no Scriptural evidence of the change of the Sabbath institution from the seventh to the first day of the week." Notice his concluding thought—"What a pity that Sunday comes branded with the mark of paganism, christened with the name of the sun god, when adopted and sanctioned by the papal apostasy and bequeathed as a sacred legacy to Protestantism."

That is quite a strong statement. Here is another one of interest by Dean Stanley, a historian, in his book, *Lectures on the Eastern Church*:

"The retention of the old pagan name, dies solas, day of the son, [Sunday] for the weekly Christian festival is in great measure owing to the union of pagan and Christian sentiment with which the first day of the week was recommended to pagan and Christian alike as the "venerable day of the sun.""

I think we are led to agree that the first day of the week is based, not on Scripture, not upon a command of our Lord, not on a "thus saith the Lord," but on tradition.

We have prayed that God will open our minds and help us know His will—to help us see the light as it shines upon our pathway—and I believe He has answered our prayer. For a moment we must take one more look in the Old Testament, for I want to show you that God is never caught unaware. God foresaw this change centuries before it came about. The book of Daniel was written about 700 years before Christ. Daniel described a vision that he had, in which he saw an apostate power that was to arise. Notice his description: "He shall speak pompous words against the Most High, shall persecute the saints of the Most High, and shall intend to change times and law" (Daniel 7:25).

Through the prophet Daniel, God said that a religious power would arise and actually seek to change God's law. We can see that is exactly what happened. A religious power arose in the form of the apostate church and sought to put as the day of worship—in place of the day that God had given—a manmade institution. Is it any wonder that Jesus said during His ministry that "in vain do they worship me, teaching for doctrines, the commandments of men" (Matthew 15:9)?

How soon did Sunday come into the Christian church? The first mention of Sunday as a day of Christian worship comes from Justin Martyr, in Rome, A.D. 150—nearly half a century after the last book of the New Testament was written. Moreover, this was not a command but simply a mention of the first day of the week made by one man in a specific locality.

Later, in A.D. 321, the pagan Roman emperor, Constantine, passed a civil statute setting aside Sunday as a civil day of rest. That was the first civil Sunday law, but it was not the last.

How long before Sunday became common Christian practice? Socrates, a historian in the fifth century (not to be confused with Socrates the Greek philosopher), wrote in A.D. 440:

"Although almost all churches throughout the world celebrate the sacred mysteries [or Lord's Supper] on the Sabbath every week, yet the Christians at Alexandria and at Rome, on account of some ancient tradition, have ceased to do this."

Did you catch the significance of that statement? For nearly five centuries almost all Christians of the world were still keeping the Sabbath, except at Rome and Alexandria, the very places where this compromise began.

Someone may argue, "That's all clear, but one thing bothers me. How about all of the Christians who have lived and died earnestly and honestly keeping another day? What is God going to do with them?"

Let's say a lady goes to a store to buy some yardage. The store owner measures it off on the counter, and the lady takes it home and stretches it out on the floor and lays a pattern out on it. But it won't quite fit, and she thinks, "Why, that's strange. I wonder why that is." Then she turns the pattern all around, but it just won't go on that material.

So she wraps it all up and puts it in the bag and takes it back to the store. Laying it down on the counter, she says, "You shortchanged me." The man is embarrassed and says, "I am terribly sorry—let's see." Then he stretches it out on the yardstick there and it measures just right.

Now, she is embarrassed, so she takes it back home feeling rather crestfallen and stretches it out on the living room floor again and carefully places it just as the instructions say. But, lo and behold, it comes out short again. She just cannot figure it out. So she gets out a yardstick and she measures it. Sure enough, according to her yardstick, it's short.

She wraps the material again and this time, with the material under one arm and the yardstick under the other, she marches back down to the store, saying, "This is short! I measured it by my own yardstick."

So the store owner lays her yardstick out on the counter with his and finds that they are a different length. So who is right? The only thing they can do is to have a man from the Bureau of Standards come and, with an official yardstick, measure to see which one is right. Sure enough, the one that was built into the counter years ago is short.

At this point the man who owns the store feels very badly, but he doesn't know the history of the store. Many years earlier, a man built the store and, in building the counter, had a yardstick built in that was intentionally short. He figured that over the course of years he could measure off material and save a little each time. That way he would be adding a little to his profit.

Some years later, he retired and willed the store to his son. The son knew nothing about the short yardstick. Hence, all during the time he owned the store, he had sold material by this short yardstick. The son later sold the store to its present owner, who also knew nothing about the shortage, and through the years he sold material there too.

So was the man guilty who built the store and built this short yard-stick into the counter in the beginning? Absolutely! The son who later inherited it and sold, as far as he knew, a good yard's worth of material every time—was he guilty? Absolutely not! He was living up to the best of what he knew—he was being an honest man. Was the present owner being dishonest up until this time? No, of course not, he thought he was giving full measure. Consider this: when the light—the awareness—comes to the owner, and he sees that the yardstick is short, now he has a new responsibility, doesn't he? That is to make a correction in his dealings. Do you see the point?

Back there in the days when the Sabbath was changed, when that short measure was put into the yardstick, the power that made the change became guilty and stands before God condemned. But for all the honest people who through the centuries have kept the manmade day, living up to truth to the best of their ability and following God to the best of their knowledge, God takes that into account. He only holds us responsible for what we know—for what we understand of His will.

All through these years, I am sure many reading these words may have been keeping Sunday, honestly and earnestly desiring to do the Lord's will. Yet, God does not count that against them. However, when the light comes, a responsibility follows, doesn't it?

The message of the three angels in Revelation 14—a message of return-ing to the Bible—is being preached with power. This is not a church or a denomination—this is a worldwide movement. Every hour of every day, "24/7," as they say, this message is being preached around the world.

Someone might say, "Well, you are still a very small group." That is very true. But being a majority in numbers does not necessarily make that majority right. When, through his studies, Columbus thought the earth was round, was he a majority? No, in fact, he was a very small minority. And even though the majority in his time believed with all their heart that the earth was flat, their false belief did not make the earth flat.

We can see the same thing with Jesus. He certainly was a minority—just one. And remember that virtually all the leaders of the church at that time said Jesus was wrong. Yes, they quoted their scriptures, but Jesus said they erred according to the scriptures. The sad thing is, that instead of checking out the Word of God, they just listened to the majority. But again, in the end, the majority was wrong. This is why we believe this book is so vitally important. As you continue reading it, check it out according to a "Thus says the Lord" and not a "Thus says the majority."

In the end I see a small group—as God's true followers always have been. In that group I see every single Bible writer, and I see every single disciple of Christ. I see Paul, the apostle, and then standing head and shoulders above all these, standing there with the prophets and the kings, I see Jesus. He is beckoning, "Come, and follow me." I would rather follow Jesus.

In that great judgment day when we are required to stand and to answer for our faith, if God looks down at me and asks, "Why did you keep the seventh-day Sabbath?" I will simply take the Bible and turn back to the book of Genesis and say, "Lord, you said the Sabbath was to be kept. You set it aside and sanctified it. Two thousand years before there was a Jewish nation, You told me that we were to keep the Sabbath."

When I start through the Scriptures, I come to the book of Exodus. "Father, there we find the instructions written by Your finger. Right in the heart of that, written in tables of stone, I find the command to keep the Sabbath, Lord."

Then as I go down through the Bible, all the way through, nowhere do I find anything to contradict this. Next, in New Testament times I find that Jesus kept the Sabbath. Also, the disciples kept the Sabbath. After Christ was crucified, after He died and was resurrected, He was here on this earth for a short period of time, but never once did He say anything about there being a change in the Sabbath. Never once did He mention anything like that.

Furthermore, the apostles lived here after Christ ascended to heaven, but never once did they mention anywhere in the New Testament that there had been a change in the day of worship. In all that the apostle Paul wrote, much of it was questioned by his enemies, but never once did they accuse him of breaking the Sabbath. The reason they didn't was because he was keeping it. We have no record of his doing any other.

Also, I looked at books like the book of Galatians, which was written because of the controversy of circumcision. If there had been any change of the Sabbath, there would have been controversy over that, as well. The Jewish nation would have been indignant, and charges would have been brought against the people of God. Yet, I find only silence.

Then I looked at the book of Revelation—the final revelation of Jesus Christ to this earth—and I read: "Here are those who keep the commandments of God and the faith of Jesus" (Revelation 14:12).

The seventh-day Sabbath has always been kept, and the Bible tells me that it is even going to be kept in heaven. Besides, those preparing for heaven are going to keep it here. Yes, Lord, I kept it because I was following your example.

But, friends, if I should deny the Sabbath and decide that it did not make any difference, then stand someday before God, suppose He asked me, "Why did you not keep the Sabbath? Why did you keep the first day of the week?" What then would my answer be? What then could I say? Everybody else did it? I didn't really think it was important? I was afraid to change? Somehow I believe that any excuse would be weak in the eyes of God.

What would be your answer?

CHAPTER 6

God's Law and His Grace —Partners or Enemies?

A few miles out of town is a little country church—the old-fashioned kind with the high steeple on top. It teaches about salvation from sin and has a particular viewpoint, or doctrine, about salvation.

Downtown is an older, large brick church with stained-glass windows. It too teaches about salvation, but it sees things quite differently from the little church out in the countryside.

Out in the suburbs is a massive mega-church with acres of parking and thousands of members attending every weekend. Salvation is taught here as well, but in a different way than the other two churches teach it.

You know, it's not really so important what this or that denomination says about salvation—or any other Bible teaching. We want the truth. After all, we are going to be saved because we followed the truth, not because we belong to a certain church or denomination. I see little use in defending this denomination or that, or in arguing over this doctrine or that doctrine, if we are not actually getting ready for heaven.

Salvation is the most important thing in this life. Nothing in all of life even begins to compare in importance with it. Jesus Himself said: "For what shall it profit a man, if he shall gain the whole world, and lose his own soul? Or what shall a man give in exchange for his soul?" (Mark 8:36, 37 KJV).

A young man went to Jesus one time, very much concerned over this question. He put the question to Jesus plain and straight: "What good thing shall I do that I may have eternal life?" (Matthew 19:16).

The answer Jesus gave him was just as plain and just as straight: "If thou wilt enter into life, keep the commandments," and then "come and follow me" (Matthew 19:17, 21).

Keep the commandments. Follow me. It is the two-fold formula from the lips of Jesus Himself. I submit to you on the basis of this statement from Jesus that anyone willing to keep God's commandments and follow Him is going to be saved—not primarily because a person keeps the commandments but rather because he or she follows Jesus. However, anyone willing to follow Jesus will certainly be unable to ignore the words of Jesus when He said, "If ye love me, keep my commandments" (John 14:15 KJV).

Millions of Christians believe that people are saved by grace this side of the cross—and they are absolutely right about that. But how were the people saved *before* the cross? If grace has been in operation only this side of the cross, there must have been a different formula for salvation before the cross. Were people back then saved because they kept the law? Many people think so, but just imagine what a division that would cause in heaven.

Suppose in heaven you are walking down the street of the Holy City and you see a man by the name of Abraham, and you sit down to talk with him. Jesus said we would do just that. "And I say unto you, that many shall come from the east and west, and shall sit down with Abraham, and Isaac, and Jacob in the kingdom of heaven" (Matthew 8:11 KJV).

"Well, Abraham, I'm glad to meet you. I have read about you many times in the Bible and have looked forward to talking with you. Tell me, how did you get into heaven?"

"Why, I got here because I kept the law."

"Oh, you kept the commandments?"

"Yes, I kept them meticulously, in every little detail. I kept them so well that God permitted me into the kingdom. How did you get here? You must have kept the commandments, too."

"No, sir! I didn't keep the commandments."

"You didn't keep the commandments—and you are here in heaven?"

"That's right. You see, I lived in New Testament times, and we didn't have to keep God's commandments. All we had to do was love, love, and then love some more. We didn't have to pay any attention to the commandments."

Do you see what a difference that would make in heaven? Some people would be there because they really worked hard and kept the commandments, and some people would be there because they didn't do anything. They just loved.

Do you think there will be divisions like that in heaven? Do you? Not for a minute! Why, Paul himself said: "For the grace of God that bringeth salvation hath appeared to all men" (Titus 2:11 KJV).

To how many men? All men. Was Adam a man? Was Abraham a man? Then God's grace was revealed to them—and they lived in Old Testament times! Such a statement really is not strange when you stop to think of it. You would think that God would reveal His grace to man just as soon as it was needed, would you not? God is that way. In fact, He has bound Himself by promise that whenever a real need arises, He will be on hand to supply that need. He says: "My God shall supply all your need according to his riches in glory by Christ Jesus" (Philippians 4:19).

When was grace first needed? Why, Adam and Eve needed it way back there in the Garden of Eden, didn't they? They received it, too. Yet, I want to show you something that very, very wonderful, something that illustrates the promise made by Isaiah, when he wrote: "It shall come to pass that before they call, I will answer; and while they are yet speaking, I will hear" (Isaiah 65:24).

The Bible shows that this grace, revealed in the plan of salvation, God made ready in case the need should ever arise, and long *before* man was ever created. "Who hath saved us, and called us with an holy calling, not according to our works, but according to his own purpose and grace, which was given us in Christ Jesus before the world began" (2 Timothy 1:9 KJV).

Think of it. In a solemn covenant between God the Father and God the Son, way back in the days of eternity, the death of Christ was agreed upon as a surety of redemption for the human race in case it should ever be needed. This was done before man was created. Thus, it is that Jesus is referred to in Revelation as the "Lamb slain from the foundation of the world" (Revelation 13:8).

As soon as our first parents sinned and the condemnation of death rested upon them, their Creator hastened to reveal His grace to them that very day. Have you ever wondered why Adam and Eve didn't die the very day they sinned? God had said, "For in the day that thou eatest thereof thou shalt surely die" (Genesis 2:17 KJV).

Two questions: First, why did death have to be arbitrarily administered for their sin? Second, why did they not die that very day if that was what God said would happen?

As to the first question—it has seemed to many that death was too severe and arbitrary. Why did it have to be? We must remember that God is the Source of life. From Him emanates the power that keeps every living thing alive. It is His constant power that keeps the worlds in their orbits, that keeps our hearts beating, and that keeps the organs of our bodies functioning.

For Adam and Eve to sever themselves from that Source of life was to incur the sure result of death—and that was not the result of an arbitrary decree from God. It was as natural for them to die as for a limb of a tree to die when severed from the main trunk. When Adam and Eve chose to obey the enemy of God and disobey God, they severed themselves from the Fountainhead of life and put themselves under servitude to the devil.

The devil could promise them everything but could deliver to them nothing but death.

Why did they not die that day? They should have died, and would have, had nature taken its course. In fear of that, Adam and Eve hid themselves in the Garden of Eden that day when they heard the voice of God calling them. They thought their time had come to die, and they were afraid.

"Oh, Adam," said Jesus, "I have not come to kill you. I have come to give you hope." On that very first day of sin, Jesus announced to our first parents the plan of grace. He told them how He, the Creator, would suffer the penalty of transgression, so that Adam and Eve and all their posterity could be saved. Then to show them something of what it meant for the innocent to die for the guilty, the lives of animals were taken that very day. The Bible says, "God made coats of skins and clothed them" (Genesis 3:21 KJV).

I don't think they did any boasting about those fur coats, do you? No, sir! If in that hour of sorrow they found cause to rejoice over anything, it was over the message of grace they had received—the message of grace that salvation had been provided for the guilty.

Yes, "the grace of God that bringeth salvation hath appeared to all men" (Titus 2:11 KJV). It was preached first in the Garden of Eden, and it has been preached by the ministers of God in every generation since. It hasn't made one bit of difference whether men lived in the Old Testament times or in the New Testament era. They have all needed the grace of God, and they have all received it in exactly the same way. The need was the same, and the remedy was the same. "Wherefore, as by one man sin entered into the world, and death by sin; and so death passed upon all men, for that all have sinned" (Romans 5:12 KJV). "For as in Adam all die, even so in Christ shall all be made alive" (1 Corinthians 15:22 KJV).

To understand this makes the Old Testament a gloriously new book. Those who begin learning of the life of Jesus at Bethlehem's manger—or the preaching of grace as being only on this side of the cross—miss the real Christ of the Bible. He is all through the Old Testament as well, and to understand this gives meaning and depth to the Bible story that would otherwise be missed. This is the key to the Bible, and Satan would have us miss this key.

Long before video games came along, I read the story of a man coming home from work one night. He'd had a particularly heavy day and did not feel up to wrestling with his two lively young sons, who he knew were just waiting for him to come through the door. On the way home, he stopped and bought a jigsaw puzzle for the boys. He thought that perhaps it would keep them occupied for the evening and would enable him to relax with the evening paper. The puzzle was a map of North America.

"Boys, I've brought you something," he announced as soon as he stepped in the house. "As soon as supper is over, I will show it to you."

The boys, of course, were delighted with the puzzle, and as they tackled the job of putting together the myriad pieces of North America, the father settled back in his easy chair, feeling very pleased with himself over the idea. He had not been there fifteen minutes before the boys came running in.

"Look, Dad, we have it all put together!" His heart sank.

"How in the world did you get that map put together this quick?"

"Oh," they said, "it was easy." On the other side of the puzzle they had discovered another picture—a picture of Uncle Sam. The boys had just turned it over and put the man together, and when the man was put together, the pieces of the map were in their right places.

So there is a Man in the Bible. If we focus on Him and see Him in His proper perspective, the Bible is understandable and has new meaning. God's message of grace through the sacrifice of His dear Son was preached to Old Testament characters just as well as it was ever been preached to those of the New Testament. When the Son of God was hanging on the cross for the sins of mankind, His arms were outstretched on that cross, one arm pointing backward to the Old Testament—the other pointing forward to the New Testament. People in the Old Testament had to look forward in hope to His sacrifice, and we in the New Testament look backward in gratitude to His death. There at the foot of the cross all people of all ages receive that grace that alone cleanses from sin.

Jesus said: "If I be lifted up from the earth, will draw all men unto me" (John 12:32 KJV). Yes, in heaven people from the Old Testament and the New will sing the same song of praise: "Unto Him that loved us, and washed us from our sins in His own blood" (Revelation 1:5 KJV).

So all men are saved by grace. But many may question, "Why the vast difference between Old Testament worship and worship in the New Testament?" People in the Old Testament were required to follow certain laws that we do not have to follow in the New Testament. Why this great difference if we are saved in the same way?

To understand this is truly important for us. Right here exists one of the greatest misunderstandings of modern Christendom. It is because of a misunderstanding on this point that multitudes of honest Christians lay aside the Sabbath of the fourth commandment on the assumption that it is Jewish, belongs to the Old Testament rituals, and therefore came to an end when Christ died on the cross.

Please follow me closely. The Bible speaks of a law that was added because of transgression. Paul mentions it in Galatians 3:19: "Wherefore then serveth the law? It was added because of transgressions" (KJV).

This law that was added did not exist before sin came along. It was added to meet the emergency of sin and was obviously of a temporary nature. There was also a law that came to an end at the cross of Christ. This was the law Christ nailed to His cross and was forever abolished by His death: "Blotting out the handwriting of ordinances that was against us, which was contrary to us, and took it out of the way, nailing it to his cross" (Colossians 2:14 KJV).

This law that was added, or brought into being because of sin, is the same law that came to an end at the cross of Christ. It had nothing to do with God's everlasting Ten Commandments. The Ten Commandments are a perfect photograph or reflection of God's character and are as everlasting as God Himself. They did not come into being because of sin and will never throughout eternity be done away with or abolished.

Remember, the very day Adam and Eve sinned, the blood of animals was shed. Our first parents walked out of the Garden of Eden clothed with the skins of the animals whose lives were shed because of sin. This was the beginning of the long centuries of blood sacrifices that were offered in the Old Testament. The animals were not to blame for man's sins. Yet, those animals had to die. Why was that? It was a powerful lesson to the repentant sinner that he, the sinner, could go free because an innocent sacrifice was dying in his place.

It wasn't possible, of course, for those animals to atone for sin. The Bible says, "For it is not possible that the blood of bulls and of goats should take away sins" (Hebrews 10:4 KJV).

Those animals were only a symbol or an illustration to men that the Son of God—the innocent victim—was to come down and die in their place. Yet, there was no other way for men in the Old Testament to show their faith in the promised Redeemer. Not to offer the sacrifice was to deny the blood atonement of their Redeemer and thus cut themselves off from their only hope of salvation.

Hence, when Cain and Abel offered their sacrifices before God, Cain's sacrifice was rejected and Abel's was accepted. Why? It was because there was no blood in Cain's sacrifice. His was a manmade religion, and like all manmade religions since, it sought to improve a little bit on God's religion. The Bible says that Cain brought to God the fruits of the ground. I suppose he offered some lovely flowers, or perhaps some beautiful peaches or bananas—fruits that grew right next to the Garden of Eden. I suppose that, as far as the eye of man could tell, it was an even lovelier gift than the bloody sacrifice of Abel, but the Bible says that God despised Cain's offering.

There was Cain, the first modernist of all time, declaring, "I'll be religious. I believe in a good moral life. I believe in philosophy, in education, and in every good thing, but don't talk to me about a blood atonement. I don't need it and don't want it." As a result, his offering did not pass. God despised and rejected it.

Abel offered a sacrifice with blood, showing his faith and dependence upon the shed blood of his Redeemer. God was pleased with Abel's sacrifice and accepted it.

Thus, down through the ages men in the Old Testament indicated their faith in their Redeemer to come by their offerings of blood upon their altars. It was a worship of symbols and ceremonies, and it was a temporary system to illustrate salvation until the Redeemer should actually come.

This was the law that was added because of transgression. It was commanded by God, and a man could not be saved back in Old Testament times without following its ritual. Thus those millions of sacrifices offered at that time all had a meaning. Christ was the center of it all—the same Christ and the same blood atonement that we look to today.

Why were they required to follow this ritual before the cross, and we are not required to follow it this side of the cross? It is simple because in the Old Testament, the first coming of Christ was still future. It was not given to men to look into the future the way they can look to the past. Because it was extremely important that people never lose sight of this heaven-sent provision of their Redeemer, God "added this law" of symbols and ceremonies, the very carrying out of which would keep before them the sure and certain promise of a Redeemer to come. God knew men would lose sight of the promise unless they had something tangible to follow. The rituals of the ceremonial law provided something tangible to keep their focus on the right track.

Paul compared these ordinances and ceremonies to a "shadow of things to come; but the body," he said, "is of Christ" (Colossians 2:17 KJV).

If you follow the shadow of a pole, even though you do not look up to see the pole, by following the shadow you will be led unerringly to the foot of that pole. But on the other side of the pole there is no shadow.

After 4,000 years of promise, the promise finally came to pass: "When the fulness of the time was come, God sent forth His Son, made of a woman, made under the law" (Galatians 4:4 KJV). John the Baptist also stopped short in his preaching one day when he saw Jesus and exclaimed: "Behold the Lamb of God, which taketh away the sin of the world" (John 1:29 KJV).

So too it was that when Jesus died upon the cross, He cried out with a loud voice, "It is finished." What was finished? That long period of ceremonies and rituals had been in effect since the first day of sin, and at last it had all come to an end. As Jesus died on the cross, by a supernatural display of power, God tore the veil of the temple in two—from top to bottom. The temple service on this earth was forever ended.

> "Which was a figure for the time then present, in which were offered both gifts and sacrifices … which stood only in meats and drinks, and divers washings, and carnal ordinances, imposed on them until the time of reformation." (Hebrews 9:9, 10 KJV)

> "Blotting out the handwriting of ordinances that was against us, which was contrary to us, and took it out of the way, nailing it to his cross … Let no man therefore judge you in meat, or in drink, or in respect of an holyday, or of the new moon, or of the sabbath days: *which are a shadow of things to come; but the body is of Christ.*" (Colossians 2:14, 16, 17 KJV, emphasis added)

All the sacrificing of animals—all the new moon and yearly feasts that were called ceremonial Sabbaths—came to an end, for their whole purpose was to point forward to Christ. When Christ came and died on the cross, all the ceremonial precepts of the law of Moses died with Him.

Men will agree to this, but here is where the majority make a mistake. In order to get rid of the Sabbath of the fourth commandment, they endeavor to nail the whole of God's Ten Commandments to the cross, along with all the ceremonies and ordinances of the law of Moses. This cannot be done. The Ten Commandments stand separate and distinct as God's everlasting principles of righteousness. They must not be confused with the ceremonial law. These great principles of the Ten Commandments were not added because of transgression. They were here long before sin began—from eternity.

Go down through the list of the Ten Commandments, and you cannot conceive of a time when a single one of them did not exist. Neither did they end when Jesus died on the cross. There never has been a moment in all the history of the world when it was proper and right to worship other gods, make graven images, take God's name in vain, break the Sabbath, dishonor parents, kill, steal, commit adultery, lie, or covet—there never has been a time; there never will be. Even in eternity—the new earth—these principles will still abide.

Can you think of a time over the horizon of eternity when it may become all right to worship other gods, take God's name in vain, kill, steal, lie, or commit adultery? Of course not! Those principles of right are everlasting.

These commandments never had a beginning. They were not added because of transgression. They will never have an ending. They will not cease to be right when we get into the new earth. They are as eternal as God Himself!

Even the Sabbath—the fourth commandment of the Decalogue—will be obeyed in heaven. Did you know that? Notice this: "For as the new heavens and the new earth, which I will make, shall remain before me, saith the Lord, so shall your seed and your name remain. And it shall come to pass, that from one new moon to another, and from one sabbath to another, shall all flesh come to worship before me, saith the Lord" (Isaiah 66:22, 23 KJV).

Why will the redeemed meet from one new moon to another? We can read in Revelation 22:2 that the tree of life will have twelve kinds of fruit and yield its fruit every month. Of course, the redeemed will come from one new moon to another, or from one month to another, to partake of the fruit of the tree of life. More than that, the Bible says every Sabbath God's people will come before Him in special worship.

It is too bad that men have the antipathy toward the Sabbath that they do. God made it to be a blessing to man. He put it into the heart of His Decalogue, which He wrote Himself with His own finger. Jesus honored the Sabbath when He was upon earth. On the authority of the Word of God, it is going to be kept by the redeemed in the new earth, when sin and the marks of sin are forever removed.

People often ask, "Didn't God give the Ten Commandments to the Jews?" Yes, He did. He spoke those Ten Commandments Himself from the top of Mt. Sinai in the hearing of some two million Jews. He delivered the tables of stone to Moses, the leader of the Jewish nation, but that doesn't mean that it was the Creator's will that they (the Jews) should be the only ones to refrain from worshiping idols, committing adultery, lying, stealing, etc. Of course not! These laws have always been God's will for all mankind. He gave those commandments to the Jews because at that time they comprised His church. They were in turn to go out and teach those principles to the other nations. They failed just as a lot of professed Christians fail today.

Ministers of the gospel who ought to be warning judgment-bound men about the need for obeying God are openly proclaiming that men can with impunity break these commandments of God and still get to heaven! Men today use as the basis for their arguments texts in Galatians and Colossians where Paul speaks of the law being abolished. He speaks just as plainly of the law being established in Christ. Either Paul was speaking of two different laws, or he was hopelessly confused in his theology. However, Paul was not confused; neither was the Holy Spirit confused when He dictated those affirmations to Paul. Men today are confused when they try to abolish God's holy commandments by nailing them to the cross with the ceremonial laws of Moses—that is where the confusion lies.

In Deuteronomy the fifth chapter, God lists the Ten Commandments as they are given earlier in the twentieth chapter of Exodus. Then, at the conclusion, He says: "These words [the Ten Commandments] the Lord spake unto all your assembly in the mount out of the midst of the fire … and He *added no more*. And He wrote them in two tables of stone …" (Deuteronomy 5:22 KJV, emphasis added).

There were Ten Commandments—no more, no less—written on tables of stone. The workmanship and writing was accomplished by God Himself. "The tables were the work of God, and the writing was the writing of God, graven upon the tables" (Exodus 32:16 KJV).

I think we ought to settle it right here that God knows how to count to ten. He is the great enumerator. He keeps track of the untold millions of worlds, and when He gives the Ten Commandments and then says, "That's all—I have added no more," then I think we ought to believe Him. How does it come that men will add to those Ten Commandments all the scores and scores of precepts and ordinances and ceremonies as given in the law of Moses? To do so is to call God a liar. He said He added nothing to the ten, and we would do well to believe Him.

Strange situation indeed! Think of it! Man lost his home in the beginning and his relationship with God because of disobeying a commandment of God. Has God changed? Does He look upon disobedience with more tolerance today than He did in the beginning? Hardly! He warns us about that: "I am the Lord, I change not; therefore ye sons of Jacob are not consumed" (Malachi 3:6 KJV).

With Him, there "is no variableness, neither shadow of turning" (James 1:17 KJV).

How then do you think the Almighty looks upon this action of puny man, who with boldness and perfect freedom takes God's holy commandments and shuttles them around to suit his own whims and fancies—nails them to the cross, keeps the ones he wants, and throws out the one he doesn't want! It is bad enough that men do it, but for ministers of the gospel to get into the sacred desk and teach other men to do it is a thousand times worse. Jesus said, "Whosoever therefore shall break one of these least commandments, and shall teach men so, he shall be called the least in the kingdom of heaven" (Matthew 5:19 KJV).

Didn't Jesus come to change things and to put us under grace? Jesus did come to change things, but we had better have it clear what the things were that He came to change. Certainly, it was not the everlasting principles of right as embodied in the Ten Commandments. Rather, it was the ceremonial laws of sacrifices and ordinances that were added because of transgression and that pointed forward to Christ. However, when the Christ toward which they pointed had come and completed His work, that temporary law was no longer needed. It came to an end. He nailed it to His cross. But the moral precepts of the Ten Commandments were not changed one iota by the death of Jesus upon the cross.

So then, what does it mean to be put under grace? We here in the New Testament are saved by grace, but we have already learned that the people in the Old Testament were also saved by grace. But what, exactly, is grace? The apostle Paul wrote more about grace than any other Bible writer. So let's read what he says about it:

"But none of these things move me, neither count I my life dear unto myself, so that I might finish my course with joy, and the ministry, which I have received of the Lord Jesus, to testify the gospel of the grace of God." (Acts 20:24)

There it is! What is grace? It is the gospel. What is the gospel? It is the good news of salvation. It is the fulfillment of the promise made in the Garden of Eden—God taking the place of man and suffering the full penalty for the transgression of His holy law. That was what Jesus did. He was God revealed in human flesh, and He suffered in all respects the condemnation of the damned in order that we might be free.

Please don't make the mistake of thinking that because Jesus suffered the penalty of our transgression, that He therefore abolished God's holy principles of right and freed us from having to obey God or keep His commandments.

On the contrary, Jesus came into the world to establish the law. He said Himself that He had not come to do away with the law but to fulfill, to obey, to live out its requirements in a way that no man had ever been able to do (Matthew 5:17). Isaiah said that "he will magnify the law, and make honourable" (Isaiah 42:21 KJV).

What does it mean to magnify and make honorable? It certainly does not mean to destroy or do away with. It means just the opposite. It means that the requirements of God's holy law would be made plainer to our understanding. They would be enlarged and magnified and made understandable by the spotless life of Christ, the Son of God.

Do you know what makes the life of Christ so beautiful? Do you realize why God the Father said He was well pleased with Him—something He had never said about any man who had ever lived? It was because Christ's life was a perfect replica of God's holy law. God's law is perfect. Jesus' life was perfect. He lived the law perfectly, and His life was perfect.

Have any of you married ladies ever gone shopping and taken your husband with you? Of course you have. You know how it goes! A lady will go looking for dress material in a yardage shop. She will ask the clerk for a certain bolt of goods to be brought down, and the clerk will bring it down to the counter. And instead of just letting you look at the bolt, the clerk will flip out a whole big pile of cloth from the bolt. It always seems so unnecessary to me to unwind what looks like four or five feet of the material, when six inches should do just as well.

Anyway, the lady shopping will look at that pile, and if it doesn't suit her, the clerk brings out another bolt and flips out four or five feet of that. And then another, and then another, and after awhile, there is a tremendous pile there, almost as high as the clerk's chin.

The poor husband stands there feeling so sorry for the clerk, having to roll all that material up again, but the wife stands there just as calm as can be, looking at one and then another cloth pattern. She will moisten it a little and rub it between her fingers. Then she will announce, "I don't think I will buy any today," and will walk away as calmly as though the whole episode was of the least concern to her. She will leave the clerk to roll all that stuff up alone. The poor husband feels terrible. "Oh, please, buy at least a foot of the stuff to pay the clerk for the trouble! Or at least help her roll it up!"

But the clerk isn't to be outdone that easily.

"Wait a minute," she says. "We have this material already made up in a dress. Would you like to see it?"

"Yes, I would."

So the clerk brings out a dress all made up from that material. The wife takes just one look at it. "Oh," she says, "it is lovely! It looks nice in the yardage, but it's a thousand times nicer all made up!"

That's the way it is with the commandments of God. They are beautiful, written out on the tables of stone, but they are infinitely more beautiful as lived out in the life of Jesus. Jesus is the only man in all the annals of time who has ever kept the commandments of God perfectly. You look at His life, and it is God-like. Why? It is because the principles of the Ten Commandments are lived out perfectly and without blemish in His life. No wonder God the Father said, "Thou art my beloved Son; in thee I am well pleased" (Luke 3:22 KJV).

Oh, if we could only stand before God, righteous like Jesus! Wouldn't that be wonderful! If only God would say to us, "Thou art my beloved son. I am well pleased with you." Do you know, friend, that is exactly what is required of us. In order to walk into the kingdom of God, we have to show a life that is without blemish from the cradle to the grave. Not one single sin must appear on the records against us. Not one!

You say, "How can this be? Who, then, can be saved? Not one—not one who is outside of Christ. Here the great genius of the gospel comes into play. Jesus said, "Come unto me, all ye that labour and are heavy laden, and I will give you rest" (Matthew 11:28 KJV). "Him that cometh to me I will in no wise cast out" (John 6:37 KJV).

When we cast ourselves upon Him, He removes from us our unrighteousness and gives us in its place the perfect robe of His own pure righteousness. Thus, we stand as righteous as Jesus in the sight of God. This isn't because of any inherent goodness on our part. Rather, it is because of the inherent goodness of the Savior. Because we have a God-given Savior, we have a God-given passport to heaven. All of our sins have been placed upon Jesus. All of Jesus' righteousness has been placed upon us, and we are justified by grace. So the apostle Paul said, "Sin shall not have dominion over you: for ye are not under the law but under grace" (Romans 6:14 KJV).

No longer am I now under condemnation. I am freed from condemnation through the grace of Christ. So to me now, the law is dead, for it no longer condemns me. But am I free because of this to go out and break its precepts just because Jesus has taken me out from under its condemnation? Absolutely not!

CHAPTER 7

Baptism, Salvation, and You

"All authority has been given to Me in heaven and on earth. Go therefore and make disciples of all the nations, baptizing them in the name of the Father and of the Son and of the Holy Spirit, teaching them to observe all things that I have commanded you; and lo, I am with you always, even to the end of the age." (Matthew 28:18-20)

Many people don't see—or they minimize—the importance of baptism. They shouldn't. Jesus incorporated it into His Great Commission. He gave the same authority to baptize as He did to preach the gospel. Indeed, the two are to go hand in hand—teaching and baptizing. Decisions for baptism are the goal of teaching. It was for that reason that Jesus sent forth His disciples.

Today, there are several kinds of baptism. How many does God recognize? Here is the answer, in Ephesians 4:5: "One Lord, one faith, one baptism."

One baptism! How many methods of baptism are you aware of? I once counted fourteen. In some churches they sprinkle; in others they pour. One church baptized the candidate three times, face downward, in the name of the Father, Son, and Holy Spirit. Some churches baptize by a single immersion. I read once of a minister who baptized with rose petals. Sometimes salt is used. In one church where babies were being baptized, the minister took the infant into his arms and just laid his dry hand on its head and pronounced, "I baptize you in the name of the Father, and of the Son, and of the Holy Ghost." Without one drop of water! That should probably be called the dry cleaning method. Babylon! Confusion!

People will tell you sometimes that the actual method does not make any difference, just so the heart is in it and you are sincere. But do not count on that. We want to be sincere, to be sure—but we want to be right, too. And the only way of being right is not necessarily what the church or some group of preachers say, but rather what the Bible says. The two ought to be synonymous, but unfortunately, sometimes they are not.

If we could just get it settled in our thinking that regardless of churches, preachers, relatives, or anyone else, we are going to do exactly what the Bible teaches and stick to that, it would solve every religious problem that has ever arisen or that ever will arise in our lives. *What does the Bible say?* Study earnestly and find out. Then, when you have your answer, don't start looking around for a way out.

Go ahead and do it. If you do, you will find a satisfaction and joy in your Christian life that you have never dreamed possible. If it takes a miracle to enable you to obey the Book, don't hesitate. Go ahead, in spite of the way things look, and you will find that heaven is still ready to perform miracles for anyone willing to obey God's Word.

Our first parents lost their Eden home because they did not believe what God said. He said, "Don't eat of this tree."

The devil said, "Now, that doesn't really matter. It is not the literal carrying out of this command that God is interested in, but rather, whether your heart is in it or not."

You know the story, of course. They believed the devil. They disobeyed God, so they lost everything.

Here is another instance—the story of two young men, preachers. God told them that only holy fire should be used in the sanctuary service. But they could not see any difference between the fire God kindled and ordinary fire. So one day they offered ordinary fire in the sanctuary. Do you know what happened? Fire came out from the altar and killed those young men right there in the sanctuary before all the children of Israel: "Nadab and Abihu died when they offered profane fire before the Lord" (Numbers 26:61).

Yes, people needed the same lessons back then. If God says, "Do it," then *do it.* If God says, "Don't do it," then *don't do it.* As I have said, the learning of that simple lesson will clear up every problem of religious befuddlement in your mind. It will clear up for you the Sabbath question. It will give you your answer about baptism. You will have a clear direction for your feet, and you will have—in addition to all that—the joy of real adventure in your soul.

By what method ought men to be baptized? I think everyone would agree that if we can find out how Jesus was baptized, we will have the right method. Let us find out how He was baptized.

The Gospel of Mark tells of when John the Baptist was preaching and baptizing in the Jordan River. Suddenly, one day a young man named Jesus went to him for baptism.

"It came to pass in those days that Jesus came from Nazareth of Galilee, and was baptized by John in the Jordan. And immediately, coming up from the water, He saw the heavens parting and the Spirit descending upon Him like a dove." (Mark 1:9, 10)

It had to have been *in* the river where Jesus was baptized, or He could not have come up *from* the water, could He? Obviously, Jesus went down into the water and was immersed there, but lest there be a lingering doubt about how John baptized, let us look at another verse: "Now John also was baptizing in Aenon near Salim, because there was much water there. And they came and were baptized" (John 3:23).

John needed a lot of water when he baptized people, but if he had baptized the way some preachers do, all he would have needed was a half gallon bucket of water, and he could have baptized 2,000 people out there in the desert. But John needed a lot of water—deep water for people to be immersed.

In one church I read about, a little girl about 12 years old wanted to be baptized. This happened to be in a church where the candidates for baptism were given the privilege of choosing how they were to be baptized—by immersion or sprinkling. Several adults were to be baptized in addition to this little girl. One reason I like this story is because it illustrates how much children get out of the Bible. Sometimes, they get a lot more out of it and get the meaning a lot straighter than we adults do.

Anyway, as the minister and his associates were walking down the line of people, getting the name of each one and asking how he or she wanted to be baptized, almost every one of them preferred to be sprinkled—probably because it was less trouble. As the minister came to this little girl, he asked, "Honey, how would you like to be baptized?"

"I want to be baptized just like Jesus was baptized," she replied. That was a good answer, wasn't it? The minister turned to his associates and said, "We will have to take her down to the river." That minister would not have dared sprinkle that little girl, when her request was to be baptized just as Jesus had been.

So what is the meaning of baptism? To understand that is to understand a mighty reason why baptism by immersion is the only method God will recognize in the judgment.

"Therefore we were buried with Him through baptism into death, that just as Christ was raised from the dead by the glory of the Father, even so we also should walk in newness of life." (Romans 6:4)

What does it say baptism is? It is a burial. And how do we bury people? We put them completely under, don't we? If, after the funeral, our dead were buried the way people are buried with their Lord in baptism by some churches, there would be a protest and scandal that would sweep the nation. Just imagine people being buried with a little dirt sprinkled over them. Yet, that is exactly the meaning of baptism. It is a burial service. Again, we read in Colossians 2:12: "Buried with Him in baptism, in which you also were raised with Him through faith in the working of God, who raised Him from the dead."

How do we normally bury a person—face up, or face down? Face up, true? Do we bury them once, or three times, on the day of the burial? Just once. Please get this picture. Here is a minister with the baptismal candidate. They both go down into the water. The candidate stops breathing. He closes his eyes. He is just like a dead person. Then the minister gently lays him back under the water so that he is completely buried. Then the minister lifts him up. The candidate begins to breathe—he opens his eyes and begins to move. He has come to life again.

Baptism by single immersion is the only kind that carries out the symbol of a death, a burial, and a resurrection. That is exactly what baptism is designed to be. It commemorates the death, burial, and resurrection of Christ, and it also symbolizes the sinner's dying to the old way of life, his burial of the old man of sin, and his rising from the watery grave to walk in newness of life.

I might say right here that only people who truly are dead ought to be buried. By the same token, only people who truly are converted should be baptized. It doesn't do one bit of good for a person to be dunked under the waters of baptism unless his or her heart has been changed. A heart experience must take place before baptism can mean anything. Once that experience has taken place, and the person has dedicated his heart to the Lord Jesus, then the next step is baptism. It signifies death to the ways of the world, and the old man of sin is buried; moreover, it is terrible for a person to be buried when he is not dead.

I read a story some time ago about a young lady in the state of Virginia who was taken ill. In spite of all the doctors could do, she grew steadily worse and died. Or at least they thought she did. They had the funeral service and took her to the cemetery. Fortunately, she was buried in one of those cemeteries where people are buried on top of the ground. They put the casket in a crypt on top of the ground and left. It was to be sealed within a day or so.

But that night, the caretaker of the cemetery heard strange noises coming from that grave. He quickly called for help and opened it up and to their amazement, the workers found the young lady still alive. She actually had not died. They took her home, and believe it or not, she recovered. Later on, she was married and had a son. The name of her son is known all over the country—Robert E. Lee.

Yes, a burial service should only be conducted for people who are dead, and a baptismal service should only be conducted for people who have died to the world. That does not mean that the person being baptized has to have arrived at a place where he can no longer be tempted. It does mean, however, that he has committed his life and soul to Christ. When that is done, a life from outside this world is implanted within him, and the old man of sin is dead. Therefore, the burial service of baptism is appropriate and important.

The word "baptize" is actually a Greek word that has been anglicized. The word in the original Greek is *baptizo*. The New Testament was written in Greek, and as the record was written down of the institution of baptism, it was natural that it be called *baptizo*. Then, as the gospel went into other countries, the languages in these countries had no religious service that was equivalent to *baptizo* in the Greek, so the name was just incorporated into the language wherever the gospel was preached. We have anglicized it, and we call it "baptize," but it is exactly the same word as *baptizo*, and it means exactly the same thing. *Baptizo* in Greek means exactly what our words "immerse" and "submerge" mean. It means "to put completely under." Thus, it has been a symbol through the years of a burial and a resurrection.

In the Old Testament, God's people had many kinds of ordinances they were to follow. God gave these ordinances, and He meant for each to be carried out in just the way He commanded. As we noted in the previous chapter, in the New Testament God gave only two ordinances—the communion service and baptism. Both of these services have been changed by men, but do not think that God will be any more pleased with a change of His commandments in the New Testament than He was with changes to what He commanded in the Old Testament.

When someone has been baptized, he has done something—he has actually taken upon himself the name of the Lord Jesus Christ. "For as many of you as were baptized into Christ have put on Christ" (Galatians 3:27).

Such a person has taken the name of Christ and the life of Christ to himself, and it is a very solemn experience—something no one should take lightly. No one should expect to get through to the kingdom without it. "Jesus answered and said to him [Nicodemus], 'Most assuredly, I say to you, unless one is born again, he cannot see the kingdom of God'" (John 3:3).

When Peter was preaching on the day of Pentecost, the people listening came under deep conviction.

> "Now when they heard this, they were cut to the heart, and said to Peter and the rest of the apostles, 'Men and brethren, what shall we do?' Then Peter said to them, 'Repent, and let every one of you be baptized in the name of Jesus Christ for the remission of sins; and you shall receive the gift of the Holy Spirit.'" (Acts 2:37, 38)

Every man and woman and boy and girl should take seriously this command. We all want to be saved, so we should not fail to be baptized in the way Jesus has commanded. Only upon baptism is the Holy Spirit able to come work in His fullness.

How old should a person be before baptism? Since baptism indicates a decision made by the candidate between himself and his Savior, he obviously ought to be old enough to know what he is doing. In some respects, baptism is like a marriage. As Paul said, as many as have been baptized into Jesus Christ, have put on Christ. This is much like a bride taking the name of her husband.

A young United States airman in San Antonio, Texas, when asked if he had been baptized, scratched his head thoughtfully and said, "I think so."

That is like asking a man, "Are you married?" and then seeing him look bewildered, scratch his head and say, "I think so." People really ought to know if they are married or not, don't you think?

Another young man in the armed services who was attending evangelistic meetings wrote to his mother to ask her if he had been baptized. "Mother, have I been baptized? And if so, what church did I join?"

Just imagine writing home to one's mother and asking, "Mother, have I ever been married? And if so, to whom?"

We don't believe in child marriages in this country. When a person gets married, we believe it ought to be an intelligent decision on his or her part. The same principle ought to hold true for baptism.

Yes, children ought to be dedicated to Jesus, and I believe it is a lovely service for parents to take their tiny babies to the altar and dedicate them to the Savior. But baptism ought to be reserved for a time when the child can make the decision for himself. A child need not be an adult before he can feel the workings of the Holy Spirit on his heart. The age will differ with many children, but on an average, when children come to the age of 10, 11, or 12, they are entering the time when they can make an intelligent decision in giving their heart to Jesus and being baptized.

There are three requisites for baptism that I believe will help to clear up this matter of infant baptism. First, those to be baptized should be taught.

> "Go therefore and make disciples of all the nations, baptizing them in the name of the Father and of the Son and of the Holy Spirit, *teaching* them to observe all things that I have commanded you." (Matthew 28:19, 20 emphasis added)

How much can you teach an infant? Mothers work hard at it, but it is hard to teach them very much, isn't it? Fathers get in on it a little bit, too, but it seems as if mothers have the brunt of the job, especially at first. Some things seep into the baby's little mind, but it is pretty hard to teach them anything about the gospel. If babies are too young to teach them the gospel, they are too young for baptism, as commanded in the gospel.

Here, next, is another requisite for baptism: "He who believes and is baptized will be saved; but he who does not believe will be condemned" (Mark 16:16). How much can an infant believe? Why, they can't believe in anything outside of their own comfort, can they? Therefore, an infant should not be baptized, because it has not yet learned to believe the gospel.

Finally, let's read again in the New Testament of when Peter was preaching on the day of Pentecost:

> "Now when they heard this, they were cut to the heart, and said to Peter and the rest of the apostles, 'Men and brethren, what shall we do?' Then Peter said to them, '*Repent,* and let every one of you be baptized in the name of Jesus Christ for the remission of sins; and you shall receive the gift of the Holy Spirit.'" (Acts 2:37, 38 emphasis added)

What does Peter say the people should do? Repent. Of how much can a baby repent of? Why, it has not done anything yet for it to repent. Therefore, there is no reason for it to be baptized.

We do not need to invent a way for God to save the children. He loves them far more than we are capable of doing, and we must leave this to the One who always has a better plan and who said:

> "'Let the little children come to Me, and do not forbid them; for of such is the kingdom of God. Assuredly, I say to you, whoever does

not receive the kingdom of God as a little child will by no means enter it.' And He took them up in His arms, laid His hands on them, and blessed them." (Mark 10:14-16)

Let us compare God's method with man's method on this ordinance of baptism.

God's Method	Man's Method
• Taught to observe all things whatsoever Jesus has commanded	• Infant knows nothing
• Believe with all your heart	• Baby incapable of believing anything.
• Intelligent decision on part of candidate	• Decision on part of parents *for* the candidate
• Conversion to Christ on part of candidate	• Contract between parents and church for candidate
• Holy Spirit enters heart at once	• Godfather and godmother take over until candidate comes to age of accountability
• Symbol of a complete burial and resurrection	• A few drops of water on the head of candidate

Isn't it amazing how far apart God's method and man's method are? Yet, a vast majority of people are perfectly content to take man's method, in spite of what God has said. They say, "Well, that is what my church teaches, so I guess it will be alright." But don't count on it. God is not a man that He can be mocked or have His commands set aside for the commands of a church or a bishop.

Some say, "But you don't understand. In this matter of infant baptism, it isn't as foolish as you make it sound. In our church we have godfathers and godmothers to take over for the infant until it comes to the age of accountability."

Some churches have this practice, but where did they get their authority for such a thing? Certainly they did not find it in the Bible. The Bible is plain in declaring that not one soul can stand for another in the judgment: "'Even if these three men, Noah, Daniel, and Job, were in it, they would deliver only themselves by their righteousness,' says the Lord God" (Ezekiel 14:14).

Not even Noah, Daniel, and Job were good enough to be a godfather for anyone. How is it that the church encourages men to stand up today and assume that role? Every man and woman must stand before God, either saved or lost, on his own—depending on his personal relationship with the Savior.

How long should a person wait before being baptized? Not long. Once the decision is made to go forward with Jesus and keep His commandments, there ought not to be much time that passes before baptism.

You may conclude that I believe in a slip-shod preparation of candidates for baptism. Just the opposite! I believe that men and women should be thoroughly taught before their baptism. One of the injunctions of the Great Commission is "Teaching them to observe all things …" I believe in that, and every minister is obligated before God to heed that admonition before administering the rite of baptism.

Nevertheless, it is a mistake to conclude that the teaching process must take months or even weeks. When a man or woman makes his decision for Jesus Christ, the principles of the Christian life can very quickly be taught to him. They not only *can* be, they *should* be. If new converts are to be victorious Christians, they need the strength that baptism will bring into their lives. Once they have taken their stand for Jesus and have been taught the principles of the gospel, they should be baptized immediately. The testing process is a lifelong process. The baptism goes with their new birth.

Picture the experience of the jailer at Philippi. Paul and Silas had been preaching the gospel in that city and had been put in prison. They had been beaten, and their hands and feet were in stocks, but they did not complain. Instead, they sang songs and praised God. The Lord finally said to an angel, "Go down and turn those men loose." The angel did, and as he approached the earth, there was a great earthquake and the prison doors swung open. The stocks fell off, and the men were free. When the jailer learned what had happened, he went to them and besought these ministers, "Sirs, what must I do to be saved?" (Acts 16:30).

Paul and Silas, true to their commission, gave him the gospel. Maybe he had heard them preach before they had been put in jail and had come under conviction. The Bible does not say, but I like to believe that he had. At any rate, it says that night—that very night, mind you—that jailer and his entire household were baptized.

There is something here we should think about. Not only is it possible for men to change the form of baptism so that it becomes meaningless, but even the right form of baptism can be hedged up with manmade restrictions so that the processes of salvation are slowed down, or in the lives of many people even stopped. The devil doesn't care at all what method he uses, just so sand can be thrown into the gospel mechanism and the Word of God impeded. Baptism should be administered close to the time when people reach a decision.

Another thing—when these new people are brought into the church, they ought to be treated for who they are—babes in the faith. They are not full grown yet and should not be expected to be—even though many times they outstrip in Christian zeal and fervor some of those church members who may be looked upon as pillars of the church. These new people will no doubt make mistakes. They may not immediately begin to bear their full load in the church. That does not mean that they are not converted or that they should not have been baptized.

Just imagine a baby being born into a home, and the older members of the family walking around his crib, deliberating as to whether they want to accept him or not. "I wonder how much wood he can chop. Is he going to be a drain on the family budget, or is he going to support himself? What part is he going to play in helping with the household chores?"

You have never in your life heard any family talk like that about a new baby. No! They rejoice over the baby. They send announcements all over the country telling of its arrival. They open their hearts to it and take it into the family without question. This ought to be no less so with new members of the church.

Some of the new babes in the church may not live, but that is no excuse for putting them on probation and treating them with distrust until they have proved themselves. Some babies die too, but we would consider it worse than criminal if they were put on probation and not given every possible chance to live.

Can baptism in itself save a person? People sometimes say, "Oh, well, it takes more than just dipping a person under the water to save him."

Let us look at that just a moment. In Old Testament times, God commanded the penitent sinner to take a lamb to the altar, confess his sins over the lamb, and take its life. Now, let me ask you a question—and you answer yes or no. Could the blood of that animal in itself save the sinner? Could it? No. Of course not! But now, could the sinner in the Old Testament be saved if he did not offer up the lamb? Yes or no? No! That is why God rejected Cain—because there was no blood in his sacrifice.

All right, we move to the New Testament times. Can lowering a person under the water in itself save that person? No, never! But, can the sinner today be saved if he doesn't go under the water in baptism? Yes or no? No! Don't be afraid of it. Baptism is absolutely imperative for all who want to be saved. Consider these verses:

- Mark 16:16: "He who believes and is baptized will be saved; but he who does not believe will be condemned."

- John 3:5: "Jesus answered, 'Most assuredly, I say to you, unless one is born of water and the Spirit, he cannot enter the kingdom of God.'"

- 1 Peter 3:21: "There is also an antitype [symbol] which now saves us—baptism (not the removal of the filth of the flesh, but the answer of a good conscience toward God), through the resurrection of Jesus Christ."

Abundantly evident is that the Bible puts a lot of importance on the rite of baptism. For anybody to minimize its importance, either for themselves or for anyone else, is a mistake.

Sometimes, people ask the question, "Should a person be rebaptized if he has been baptized by immersion once?"

The answer depends on how the person has followed the Lord since his baptism. When people are separated by divorce, it is necessary to be remarried if they are to live together again. The same principle should apply to baptism. If the person has failed to follow Christ in his baptismal vows and has gone off into the world, then he should be rebaptized when he starts following Christ again. If the person has been a Christian since his baptism, he can come into the church on his former baptism. Our church recognizes the immersion baptism of other churches. However, even in such cases, many people would be stronger if they were rebaptized and publicly renewed their commitment to Christ.

Any person who accepts Jesus takes upon himself a new nature. He lays aside the old habits of sin that belong to the family of Adam and takes upon himself the principles of the family of God.

Here is a person coming to the water's edge to be baptized. The minister asks, "What is that in your pocket?"

"Just a package of cigarettes."

"Oh, those don't belong with the family of God. Leave them on this side of your baptism."

So the person leaves them behind and goes forward to walk in the newness of life.

Another person comes to the baptism with a flask of whiskey in his pocket.

"What is that in your pocket?"

"A flask of whiskey."

"But, brother, that habit cannot enter into the family of God. You will have to leave it behind on this side of your baptism."

So he lays aside his drinking and goes forward to victory in Christ.

A girl comes tripping up with a magazine under her arm.

"What magazine is that under your arm?"

"*My True Confession* magazine."

"But don't you know that if you are going to be a Christian, you can't feed your mind with stuff like that? That has no part with the family of God. It belongs to the family of Adam. Leave it on this side of your baptism."

She lays it aside and goes forward to victory in Christ.

The great danger many people face in this matter is the habit of putting off their decision. If men and women could only realize the danger of delaying for even one day this all-important decision for eternal life, it would change the lives of so many.

How flimsy—how utterly worthless—will our excuses for delay seem when we stand before God in judgment. God said, "Today, if you will hear [My] ... voice, harden not your hearts as in the rebellion" (Hebrews 3:15).

CHAPTER 8

What Comes after Death?

P eople just do not like to talk about dying. As a friend and I walked along the streets of New York City near Times Square, we talked with the teen gang members we found on the streets. We found one group that was exceptionally well-dressed and conducting themselves in a normal way. After talking for a few minutes and asking some questions that encouraged them to talk, I asked, "Have you ever thought about what will happen to you when you die?"

Quickly, a girl in the group replied, "I'm not going to die anytime soon, so what's the sense of thinking about it?"

Before I could say anything, one of the boys, who seemed to be more serious than the others said, "How do you know?"

I then asked if they had young friends who had already died, and they began to name them one by one. Quickly, someone said, "Let's change the subject. How did we get started talking about dying?"

No, it is not exactly a party subject. No one ever says, "Say, come over to our house, and we'll have some orange soda and corn chips and talk about dying." That just isn't done. If you ever want to kill a conversation, just start talking about death.

None of us are born knowing what lies beyond the grave, but my Bible tells me that there is One who does know—none other than Jesus Christ Himself. He says: "I am He who lives, and was dead, and behold, I am alive forevermore. Amen. And I have the keys of Hades and of Death" (Rev. 1:18).

The word "hell," as used here, simply means the grave. Jesus has not only passed through the valley of the shadow of death, but here He says that He holds the key. He has been there. He has unlocked the mysteries, and His Word is crystal clear. As we study it together on this very important question, I am sure that by the blessing of His Holy Spirit, we will understand God's truth on this subject.

Here, we are going to read many Scripture references together, but I want to begin with the question that faces each of us: "What happens when we die?" I believe we can understand this best by understanding what God did when He created life in the very beginning. So, let us go to the Old Testament and read the record of the creation of man. "And the Lord God formed man of the dust of the ground, and breathed into his nostrils the breath of life; and man became a living being" (Genesis 2:7).

Let's translate that into a very simple mathematical equation. The body, which God created from the dust of the ground, plus the breath of life, equals a living soul. Is that right? Notice there must be two things to have a living soul—the body plus the breath of life. Either one by itself is NOT a living soul. Both must be there. This is what God did when He created man. Then, what happens when we die? "Then the dust will return to the earth as it was, and the spirit will return to God who gave it" (Ecclesiastes 12:7).

What did God do when He created man? He took the body plus the breath and made a living soul. When we die the body goes back to the dust from which it came, the breath of life goes back to God who gave it. This verse says the spirit goes back to God who gave it. What is that spirit? That is the breath of life—the same thing God placed in man at Creation. That same breath goes back to God at death. Do not allow the fact that this text uses the word *spirit* to confuse you. This word in this text is translated from the Hebrew word *ruach,* which means "breath." The body returns to the dust from which it was created, and the breath goes back to God who gave it. So what happens to the soul?

Let's go back to our mathematical equation. The body plus the breath equals the living soul (Genesis 2:7). The body minus the breath equals what? Absolutely nothing. Actually, you do not *have* a soul, you ARE a soul—and there is a difference. A soul is not some special separate entity that can exist by itself, but you ARE a living soul. Your body plus your breath makes you a living soul.

Let's illustrate this with a simple comparison. Say that I hold in my hand a small light bulb. And suppose for now that this bulb is a human body. When we connect it with electricity, which in our illustration will be the breath of life, what do we have? Light! It takes two things to make light—a bulb and electricity. Am I right? By the same token it also takes two things to make a living soul—the body plus the breath of life. When you disconnect the bulb from the electricity, what happens to the light? We say it goes out. What do we mean? Do we mean that the light goes back down the wire and outside someplace? No, that is not what we mean. We mean that the light simply ceases to exist. Exactly the same thing is true with life. The body plus the breath equals a living soul. When someone dies, the body returns to the dust from which it came. That spirit, or spark of life, the breath of life, returns to God who gave it. The soul ceases to exist.

Where did your breath of life come from? It came from God. No other source of life exists. Science has created many things in the laboratories of our day, but never life. Man cannot create life. All life comes from God. In fact, your Bible says so.

> "For what happens to the sons of men also happens to animals; one thing befalls them: as one dies, so dies the other. Surely, they all have one breath [the word *ruach* is used here]; man has no advantage over animals." (Ecclesiastes 3:19)

All life comes from God—not only your life and mine, but the life of every living creature. God is the only source of life, and therefore, the life that He gave you is the same breath of life which He gave to the beasts of the field.

Now, let us answer this question: "How much will you know after you have passed through the valley of the shadow of death?" That isn't hard. After we pass through that valley, we will know just as much as we knew before we were born. We had no consciousness before birth, and we have none after death. You see, the breath of life, which God holds and bestowed to you when your life began, that same breath of life goes back to God. It had no consciousness until it was united with your body, and it has no consciousness when it is separated from your body. The consciousness, the intelligent part of man, exists by combining the body and the breath. With this basic understanding, let's examine some texts to see if they will not be crystal clear in light of that which we have already read.

> "For the living know that they will die; but the dead know nothing, and they have no more reward, for the memory of them is forgotten. Also their love, their hatred, and their envy have now perished; nevermore will they have a share in anything done under the sun. … Whatever your hand finds to do, do it with your might; for there is no work or device or knowledge or wisdom in the grave where you are going." (Ecclesiastes 9:5, 6, 10)

Also, the prophet Job give his personal testimony about his experience—or what he expected to experience—at death. Job spoke about the second coming of Jesus. He knew that he might not live to see that great day. If he did not live to see Christ come, what did he expect to take place in the meantime? "If I wait for the grave as my house, if I make my bed in the darkness …" (Job 17:13).

Where did he expect to spend his time between his death and the second coming of Christ? In the grave. So let's us see what Jesus said about it in the Gospel of John: "Do not marvel at this; for the hour is coming in which all who are in the graves will hear His voice and come forth" (John 5:28, 29 first part).

Where did Jesus say they would be? They would be in the grave—all of them—both the righteous and the wicked. The rest of verse 29 says: "… and come forth—those who have done good, to the resurrection of life, and those who have done evil, to the resurrection of condemnation."

At death, we all go to the grave and await the resurrection day. The apostle Paul taught about this same thing. As we read these verses together you will notice some interesting words:

> "Behold, I tell you a mystery: We shall not all sleep, but we shall all be changed—in a moment, in the twinkling of an eye, at the last trumpet. For the trumpet will sound, and the dead will be raised incorruptible, and we shall be changed. For this corruptible must put on incorruption, and this mortal must put on immortality." (1 Corinthians 15:51-53)

I want to point out several things in this verse. First of all, notice in verse 51, Paul says "we shall not all *sleep*." Did you notice that word? Keep it in mind, for we will notice it again. In verse 52, he says that the resurrection will take place at the last trump. When is that? It will occur at the second coming of Jesus Christ, in power and great glory. Verse 53 then says: "This corruptible must put on incorruption, and this mortal must put on immortality." To be corruptible means to be subject to decay. To be *incorruptible*, then, means that we are *not* subject to decay. To be mortal means that we are subject to death and to be immortal means that we cannot die.

I need to ask another question: "Are we corruptible or incorruptible?" We are corruptible, for Paul says we will receive incorruption at the second coming of Jesus. Another question: Right now, are we mortal or immortal? Mortal, of course. When will we receive immortality? Again, it will occur at the second coming of Jesus. This is obvious from these passages of Scripture: "But I do not want you to be ignorant, brethren, concerning those who have fallen asleep, lest you sorrow as others who have no hope" (1 Thessalonians 4:13).

Notice Paul's next argument here—and I think it is beautiful: "For if we believe that Jesus died and rose again, even so God will bring with Him those who sleep in Jesus" (1 Thessalonians 4:14).

Do you believe that Jesus died and rose again? Of course you do, and Paul said that our hope in the resurrection is just as certain as the resurrection of Jesus. If Jesus died and rose again, then all who sleep in Jesus will also be resurrected. When? Verse 16 says: "For the Lord Himself will descend from heaven with a shout, with the voice of an archangel, and with the trumpet of God. And the dead in Christ will rise first" (1 Thessalonians 4:16).

Yes, if we die before God's Son comes, we need have no fear whatsoever. We can have the positive assurance of God's Word that we will simply fall asleep. We will be totally unconscious of the passing of time, and it will seem as but an instant when we will hear the trumpet of Christ and His mighty voice calling us forth to immortal life.

You may say that this sounds different from what you've been taught all your life. I realize that, but I want you to know what *God* says. Listen. Can there be any greater authority on this than Jesus Christ? What did He say about death? Let us read the record given by John. You will remember the story of the death of Lazarus, the brother of Mary and Martha—and a very close friend of Jesus. Perhaps when you have read this story previously, you weren't thinking about the particular question we are discussing and therefore did not notice the relationship between these two things. But as we read it, you will follow the story with new interest, I am sure.

Lazarus was ill. His sisters became very concerned for his well-being. Jesus was not there. They sent a message telling Him to come quickly, for His friend was sick. But Jesus was delayed in going. His disciples knew that He had received this message. They knew that Lazarus was sick. After several days, He made a statement, and we will read it in John 11:11, 12: "These things He said, and after that He said to them, 'Our friend Lazarus sleeps, but I go that I may wake him up.' Then His disciples said, 'Lord, if he sleeps he will get well.'"

Why did they say that? What did they know? They knew that Lazarus was sick. They knew that the message had come from his sisters that he was ill, so when Jesus said, "Our friend Lazarus sleeps," they reasoned, "Lord, if he sleeps he will get well."

But notice the next verse: "However, Jesus spoke of his death, but they thought that He was speaking about taking rest in sleep. Then Jesus said to them plainly, 'Lazarus is dead'" (John 11:13, 14).

What did Jesus call it? Jesus said Lazarus was asleep.

They journeyed to Bethany—a quaint little village just over the Mount of Olives from Jerusalem. A straight line of just a short distance would connect the temple in Jerusalem to the little city of Bethany. This was a favorite place for Jesus. He loved these people very much. They believed in Him. He could go into their home and have peace. They would not be bombarding Him with questions that were filled with ridicule and antagonism. He loved to be there.

When He arrived, He found a scene of great sadness. Lazarus was dead. His sisters and his neighbors and friends were mourning his death. Jesus mingled His tears with theirs, and then He asked where they had laid him. They took Him out to the tomb, and as the custom was there, Lazarus was not buried in a grave in the ground, as we usually bury people, but rather in a tomb dug into the side of a hill, with a large stone rolled in front of the tomb. The stone was round like a plate or wheel—round and flat. It was placed in a trench, and after the person had been buried in the tomb, the stone was rolled in front of the door, just as you would roll a great wheel in front of a door.

I would love to have been there when Jesus arrived at the tomb. Of all the experiences in the ministry of Christ, if I could have seen just one of them, this is the one I would like to have seen. Not only was it the site of a great miracle, but can't you see that crowd there, mourning the death of Lazarus, many of them shedding tears in mock grief and doing so only because it was customary and the polite thing to do? They could turn tears on and off like a faucet and make all the appropriate noises. Most of them did not believe or realize that Jesus had the power of resurrection, and when they followed Him out to the tomb, they wondered what He was going to do next.

Jesus made a request: "Take ye away the stone." The sisters, quick to save the Savior embarrassment, protested: "Lord, by this time he stinketh: for he hath been dead four days" (John 11:39 KJV). They knew that to roll away the stone would be unpleasant. They sought to prevent it because they loved Jesus—but Jesus insisted.

Then Jesus lifted His eyes to heaven and offered a short and simple prayer. You will find it again in the Gospel of John: "Father, I thank You that You have heard Me. And I know that You always hear Me, but because of the people who are standing by I said this, that they may believe that You sent Me" (John 11:41, 42).

I can see every eye fixed on Jesus. What was He going to do? And then, after bringing His eyes down from looking heavenward, He looked into that dark tomb and cried with a loud voice, "Lazarus, come forth!" I can see every eye looking at the tomb when Lazarus came forth. He looked like a ghost, for he was wrapped from the top of his head to the bottom of his feet in white linen. It was difficult for him to walk. He hobbled to the door of the tomb. Can't you see the look on the faces of those people? Oh, I would love to have been there that day. They stood there in utter amazement. No one spoke. No one moved. Jesus said, "Loose him." Take those things off him "and let him go." What a thrilling experience in the life of Jesus, and this teaches us something about the truth we are studying.

Jesus said, "Our friend Lazarus sleeps." The apostle Paul agreed perfectly, didn't he? And the Bible, from Genesis to Revelation, teaches the same truth—that death is an unconscious sleep. In death there is no consciousness whatever of the passing of time and events. But in perfect rest, the dead wait for the call that shall bring them forth to incorruption and immortality when Jesus comes the second time in power and great glory.

Let's read just two more verses on this point. The first is from David, and notice how he says it. He expresses it just as beautifully and adequately as we could ever hope to have it expressed: "Do not put your trust in princes, nor in a son of man, in whom there is no help. His spirit departs, he returns to his earth; in that very day his plans perish" (Psalm 146:3, 4).

There can be no question about it, can there? The Bible is universal in its teaching. It teaches the same truth from beginning to end. No contradiction exists between the Old and the New Testaments—they are a beautiful whole. The Bible teaches that death is a sleep.

You ask, "Where then did this idea come from, that when we die, we don't really die?" Most certainly, it did not come from the Bible. Do you really want to know? Its origin is not very flattering, but because we are interested in truth, we will read it together. Here is the tragic story of the sin of Adam and Eve in the Garden of Eden, when they ate the fruit God had forbidden them to eat. I want you to notice what the tempter said when he spoke to Eve:

> "Now the serpent was more cunning than any beast of the field which the Lord God had made. And he said to the woman, 'Has God indeed said, "You shall not eat of every tree of the garden"?' And the woman said to the serpent, 'We may eat the fruit of the trees of the garden; but of the fruit of the tree which is in the midst of the garden, God has said, "You shall not eat it, nor shall you touch it, lest you die."' Then the serpent said to the woman, 'You will not surely die.'" (Genesis 3:1-5, emphasis added)

Since then, the devil has been telling people that lie ever since. This idea that death is not really death, but only a change in the way of life, did not come from God—it came from Satan.

I want you to stop and think for a minute about the truth—and about how logical and reasonable it is. You see, God said plainly that He alone has immortality. This verse is important because it tells us where immortality is—and where only: "He will manifest in His own time, He who is the blessed and only Potentate, the King of kings and Lord of lords, who alone has immortality" (1 Timothy 6:15, 16).

Therefore, there can't be any doubt about that, can there be? That verse plainly says that the "blessed and only Potentate, the King of kings and Lord of lords" is the only One who has immortality. You and I may receive it at the second coming of Jesus Christ. Some people say, "But that seems like a very cold and hard thing to believe." Listen, may we talk just a moment about the practical experiences of life?

I realize full well that when you attend a funeral service these days, 99 percent of the time you will hear it said that our departed brother or sister is now in the presence of God, and that they see how we have come here to honor them. I have heard that said many, many times. People will have you believe that this is what a God of love does. But let us follow this teaching to its logical conclusion.

Suppose a mother dies. According to the common teaching, she goes to heaven. She can see everything that takes place here on this earth. She is a young mother. She leaves not only her husband to be a widower, but a six-month-old baby boy without his mother. From heaven, she can look back to this earth and watch that poor, helpless husband trying by himself to take care of a small baby boy.

Let us suppose that the boy grows up to be a drunkard. The mother sees all of this, yet heaven is supposedly a happy place where there is never a tear and never an instant of sorrow. Yet all the while, this mother must watch her husband trying to rear his motherless child. She must watch the tragedy and heartache through which they pass; yet, she must never have an instant of sorrow.

No mother who has ever lived on the earth could watch that without sorrow. That is not God's plan. God's plan is that this mother, at the moment death, falls into perfect rest. She is not conscious of anything that takes place on this earth, and she wakes at the resurrection with no consciousness of the passage of time. When we understand this, it takes away all fear. We can face death without fear, if we know God's way.

You can see that God's way is the way of infinite love—a way of perfect love and understanding. We find that we need not fear. We can know that we will rest in perfect peace until Jesus calls us to eternal life. I thank God for the resurrection and for His truth about it!

CHAPTER 9

How God Will Soon End Sin Forever

In the previous chapter, we read from the Word of God that death is an unconscious sleep in the grave—that the dead do not know anything. "For the living know that they will die; but the dead know nothing" (Ecclesiastes 9:5).

If people do not go directly to heaven or hell at death—and the Scriptures teach that they do not—then the questions, of course, come to us: "Is there a hell at all? If there is, what is it like? Is it burning now? How long will it burn? Could a God of love cast sinners into a fire? Is God a loving God? Or is He a cruel tyrant who delights in the torment of those who cross His wishes?" We will find the answers in His Book.

First, let's ask ourselves whether the doctrine of an eternally burning hell is just or even logical. Then we will find out if it is biblical.

To begin with, such a doctrine clearly is not a doctrine of love. How utterly impossible it is to reconcile the idea of a God of love with a picture of God tossing His created children into fires that never end their burning. I do not know of anyone on earth that could do that. Neither do you. Some dictator, some madman, might delight in burning his enemies, but he would not continue the torment endlessly. Yet, we have been taught that a God of love would punish a sinner for unending trillions of years and on into eternity because of a year or two or a moment or two of sin.

If people were cast into hell at death, as is widely believed, God would be guilty of executing sinners without a trial. We are enraged at the thought of punishment without trial. We seem to come into this world with a built-in sense of justice—of what is fair and what is not. God does have a day of judgment, but if people are sent to their reward or punishment at death, what need is there for a later judgment to determine their guilt or innocence? Certainly, when the Bible teaches that a day of judgment is coming when the wicked will be brought to trial, God would not execute people before

He had judged them. Therefore, you can rest assured that no one is now burning in hell. I will share with you a text in a moment that should relieve our minds of this forever.

To consign sinners to never-ending flames at death would be a most unfair act, certainly not worthy of a just God. For instance, Cain killed one man, his brother. If the never-ending hell idea is right, that would mean he has been writhing in torment now for close to 6,000 years. If some recent dictator, guilty of murdering thousands or millions of innocent people, should be consigned to the flames, he never could catch up with Cain in the amount of punishment—even though each should go on burning through all eternity. Cain still would have received 6,000 years more punishment for the murder of considerably fewer people than the dictator. Are we willing to ascribe such injustice to God?

Think again of the pictures of hell you saw as a child—of Satan standing beside the fire with a pitchfork, perhaps, tossing people in. Can we believe that if an ever-burning hell is in fact a part of God's program, He would turn over the keeping of the fire to His worst enemy? Could God trust Satan with the fires? Would He not be afraid that Satan would let the fire die down, or get too hot? Or let someone escape? What would Satan's fate be? Shouldn't Satan himself be burning if there is an eternally burning hell?

Do you see the inconsistency in the doctrine of hell as we have long been taught? Do you see how illogical it is—how it makes no sense? Our God is certainly not a God who makes decisions with less common sense than you and I use to make choices.

Where did such a doctrine originate? It simply is the natural result created by a theological misunderstanding. Satan has succeeded in convincing most of the world that when a man dies he does not die at all but is more alive than ever. Since Satan's original lie in Eden, we have been taught that man comes into the world equipped with an immortal soul that cannot die. If a man cannot die, he must go on living. If he is not good enough to live in heaven, then he will have to live somewhere else. A place in which to put these bad immortal people, therefore, became a theological need, and a never-ending hell was invented to supply that need. Such a teaching also combines well with the devil's propaganda, for from the beginning he has charged that God is a tyrant—not at all a God of love. Such a hell, if it existed, could be first-class evidence that Satan's charge against God is correct.

But, you say, the Bible speaks about hell. Christ says more about hell than anyone else in the Bible. Yes, that is right. I do not for a moment suggest that as we open the Scriptures, we will not find a hell. Yes, we will find a literal hell, with real, literal fire. Still, even in this teaching, we will find a God of love.

What does the Word actually say about hell? "The Lord knows how to deliver the godly out of temptations and to reserve the unjust under punishment for the day of judgment" (2 Peter 2:9).

So are the unjust—the wicked—being punished now? No! The Bible says the Lord is *reserving* the unjust unto the day of judgment to be punished.

The verse that gives us perhaps more information about hell than any other is Revelation 20:9: "They went up on the breadth of the earth and surrounded the camp of the saints and the beloved city. And fire came down from God out of heaven and devoured them."

We have here the account of how the wicked, after they have been resurrected (and the Bible says this happens 1,000 years after Christ's second coming), will make one last attempt to overthrow God's government. They will march against the city, the New Jerusalem, which has by then been moved to this newly recreated earth. As they are on their way to attack this city, fire will come down from heaven and destroy them.

This one text answers several of our questions. What is hell? It is the fire that God will rain down on sinners to destroy them. Where is hell? It will be right here on this earth. When is hell? It will be at the end of the thousand years that we call the millennium. Will hell burn forever? Sodom and Gomorrah, the Bible says, were destroyed with eternal fire, but are those two cities still burning today? Those two cities are mentioned as an example of how God will one day destroy the wicked. Just as He rained fire on Sodom and Gomorrah, He will rain fire upon the wicked outside the New Jerusalem. Those cities were destroyed by eternal fire, but the fire went out when it had accomplished its purpose. The fire's *effect* was eternal. The cities have never been rebuilt—have never recovered from the fire.

You may then ask, "Does not the Bible speak of unquenchable fire?" Yes, it does. "His winnowing fan is in His hand, and He will thoroughly clean out His threshing floor, and gather His wheat into the barn; but He will burn up the chaff with unquenchable fire" (Matthew 3:12).

We have unquenchable fires today that firemen are not able to control or put out with their best efforts, but the fires always go out eventually. It will be impossible to quench or control the fires of hell. However, the fires will go out when their work is done.

This is an important subject, and we want to be thorough in our study. To do this we must find all the texts in the Bible on this subject and look carefully, not superficially, at their meaning. Another text that sometimes puzzles many is Revelation 20:10, where we read: "The devil, who deceived them, was cast into the lake of fire and brimstone where the beast and the false prophet are. And they will be tormented day and night forever and ever."

This seems to say that sinners will be tormented through all eternity. But let us study it. It is speaking here of Satan. Surely Satan should be punished most and longest. Yet God says of Satan: "You have become a horror, and shall be no more forever" (Ezekiel 28:19).

Here we have what on the surface appears to be a contradiction between two verses of Scripture. Both are speaking of Satan, yet one says he will cease to exist, and the other says he will be tormented forever. Both Bible writers were inspired by the same Holy Spirit. Yet, the Holy Spirit would not contradict Himself. It must be that our understanding of one text or the other is at fault. How is this word *forever* used elsewhere in the Bible? Let's read Exodus 21:1-6:

> "Now these are the judgments which you shall set before them: If you buy a Hebrew servant, he shall serve six years; and in the seventh he shall go out free and pay nothing. If he comes in by himself, he shall go out by himself; if he comes in married, then his wife shall go out with him. If his master has given him a wife, and she has borne him sons or daughters, the wife and her children shall be her master's, and he shall go out by himself. But if the servant plainly says, "I love my master, my wife, and my children; I will not go out free," then his master shall bring him to the judges. He shall also bring him to the door, or to the doorpost, and his master shall pierce his ear with an awl; and he shall serve him forever."

The Hebrews were permitted to sell themselves as slaves, but not for life. Every seventh year, all the slaves were to go free. If a Hebrew slave had married his master's daughter, he himself could go free the seventh year, but he could not take his wife and children. If he wished to stay with his family and continue to serve his master, they could carry out a certain ceremony in which his master would bore a small hole through his ear with an awl: "... and he shall serve him forever" (verse 6).

Let's say that the slave dies. Can he still serve his master? Of course not; he will serve him only for the duration of his life on earth.

The mother of Samuel promised that she would take her son to the house of the Lord, "that he may appear before the Lord and remain there forever" (1 Samuel 1:22).

But in verse 28, his mother says: "Therefore I also have lent him to the Lord; as long as he lives he shall be lent to the Lord."

Revelation 20:10, then, does not teach eternal torment. It simply teaches us that the torment will continue as long as life lasts—as long as there is consciousness. In the parable in Luke 12:47, 48, Jesus taught that there will be degrees of punishment—that some will be punished more and longer than others, but for every soul, every lost soul, complete annihilation is the final result of the fire.

The book of Obadiah, describing the future of the nations who oppose God, teaches in verse 16 the time when the wicked would "be as though they had never been." This is the ultimate fate of those who reject the appeal of their Creator. What a loving God we have! He is not the tyrant Satan has pictured, delighting in the misery of His children, but a God who is "not willing that any should perish but that all should come to repentance" (2 Peter 3:9).

God does not want anyone to be lost. His desire is that all should be saved. He will not make us slaves, and He will not take away our power of choice. Sin and sinners must be eradicated from the universe. So those who do not choose life will not have it, but God will take no delight in their eradication. Neither will He unnecessarily prolong the punishment.

"For the Lord will rise up as at Mount Perazim, He will be angry as in the Valley of Gibeon—that He may do His work, His awesome work, and bring to pass His act, His unusual act" (Isaiah 28:21).

God's final dealing with the wicked is called His unusual act. No wonder, for what could be more difficult—more unusual or strange—for a loving Creator who longs to save every human being?

The doctrine of hell, as it is taught in the Bible, is not contrary to the concept of a God of love. Sin must be destroyed. Love could do nothing else.

Some feel that God should save everyone, regardless of a person's choice, but God will never ever do that. To save men against their will would be to fill heaven with slaves. God wants us to be residents of heaven, not slaves, or inmates, or prisoners.

Suppose that God should take a man to heaven who did not want to go? That man would look around for the tavern, or the gambling joints, or the racetracks, and he would be miserably unhappy not to find them there. Would that be love? Would it not be more kind to give that man the death he has chosen—the death toward which his sins would naturally and eventually lead?

When the picture changes, the fires that have destroyed sin and sinners will be used to purify the earth. God will restore it to its original beauty. Let's read 2 Peter 3:10-13:

"The day of the Lord will come as a thief in the night, in which the heavens will pass away with a great noise, and the elements will melt with fervent heat; both the earth and the works that are in it will be burned up. Therefore, since all these things will be dissolved, what manner of persons ought you to be in holy conduct and godliness, looking for and hastening the coming of the day of God, because of which the heavens will be dissolved, being on fire, and the elements will melt with fervent heat? Nevertheless we, according to His promise, look for new heavens and a new earth in which righteousness dwells."

God's plan for this earth will at last be carried out. He will accomplish His original purpose for it—a new earth with all sin and sinners gone.

What if someone should sometime choose to sin when all this dreadful experience with sin is over? We shall still have the power of choice, but the Bible is clear that we need have no fear that sin will ever return: "What do you conspire against the Lord? He will make an utter end of it. Affliction will not rise up a second time" (Nahum 1:9).

Sin will be ended. It will not rise up a second time to afflict us. The universe will be secured, not because we *cannot* sin, but because Calvary has taught us the horrible nature of sin. We shall not *want* to sin, for we have seen too much of its tragic results. We know what death is; we know what sickness is; we know what sorrow is—all caused by sin. Calvary will have made the universe safe. Calvary will keep it safe.

Sin, temptations, and the tempter will be gone forever. Still, the scars in the hands of Jesus will ever remind us of the price He paid to make eternity safe.

CHAPTER 10

Second and Third Arrival of the King

One time, I was speaking in Philadelphia, Pennsylvania, and a man had been attending with whom I talked about a lot of things, including end-time events. He came to the meeting one night with an entirely different concept of this subject, but at the end of the service he came up and told me that never in his life had he seen anything so clearly. Suddenly, as never before, things came together for him concerning the events before and after the return of Christ.

"You see," he told me, "I had been taught that when Jesus comes, He doesn't really come. He takes some people away, but He leaves other people here. Then later, He brings those back that He took away.

"I didn't see Him doing away with sin," he continued. "I didn't see Him doing away with death, but the Bible talks about death being done away with. So many things were confusing, but this clears up a lot of things for me."

Let's take a look at Revelation 20:1, 2: "Then I saw an angel coming down from heaven, having the key to the bottomless pit and a great chain in his hand. He laid hold of the dragon, that serpent of old, who is the Devil and Satan, and bound him for a thousand years."

This subject is sometimes called the millennium, which means "a thousand years," and a lot of different opinions exist about where and when this millennium takes place. We want to take a simple look at the Bible and see what it says, and I believe without question that if you do not try to superimpose preconceived ideas upon the Scriptures that the Bible is clear on this subject.

The book of Revelation says that an angel comes down and binds Satan for a thousand years. I've had people tell me that we are living in that millennial reign right now. Well, if that's true, then Satan must be bound with a rubber chain because he is still very active. Beyond question, we are not living in the millennium right now. But what happens when Lucifer or

Satan, the old devil, is bound for a thousand years? Let's start at the resurrection at the beginning of the millennium: "The rest of the dead did not live again until the thousand years were finished. This is the first resurrection" (Revelation 20:5).

We see here that the millennium starts with the resurrection. Many people have missed that when studying Scripture: "Blessed and holy is he who has part in the first resurrection. Over such the second death has no power, but they shall be priests of God and of Christ, and shall reign with Him a thousand years" (Revelation 20:6).

We're simply looking at Scripture verses one by one, lining up like fence posts. They point us in the direction of the truth God would have for us because we have to remember the Bible does not contradict itself. At times it may appear to, but careful study shows that it does not contradict itself. Now look at the second coming of Christ, when He returns to this earth. What we do know is this:

1. He's going to come back. This is the Second Coming.

2. At that time, He's not going to touch the earth—He calls His people up to meet Him. No problem with that at all. The Bible clearly teaches this.

3. He takes the living saints and the resurrected saints to heaven.

4. For how long? We just read that for a thousand years they will reign with Him.

Let's look at some more texts before we move on to the next point: "The Lord Himself will descend from heaven with a shout, with the voice of an archangel, and with the trumpet of God. And the dead in Christ will rise first" (1 Thessalonians 4:16).

Again, we're talking about that first resurrection: "Then we who are alive and remain shall be caught up together with them in the clouds to meet the Lord in the air. And thus we shall always be with the Lord" (1 Thessalonians 4:17).

Ever to be with Him—no separation again from the Lord—caught up in the air. That's going to be a fantastic trip. In the first resurrection we see that the righteous are resurrected. Now, what else takes place?

"Do not marvel at this; for the hour is coming in which all who are in the graves will hear His voice and come forth—those who have done good, to the resurrection of life, and those who have done evil, to the resurrection of condemnation." (John 5:28, 29)

Two resurrections—first, the resurrection of life; second, the resurrection of condemnation—we want to be a part of that first resurrection if we sleep the sleep of death before the Lord comes. We don't want to be a part of that second group. As Revelation 20:6 ways, speaking of the righteous, they will reign with Christ for a thousand years.

So what happens to the wicked? Remember that in the previous chapter on hell, we looked at this question in detail, but let's take a moment to review: "Then the lawless one will be revealed, whom the Lord will consume with the breath of His mouth and destroy with the brightness of His coming" (2 Thessalonians 2:8).

So we find that some destruction will take place at the Second Coming—no question about that. The lost are going to be destroyed by the brightness of that event. The Bible says that "every eye will see Him, even they who pierced Him" (Revelation 1:7). The Bible continues, "Then the sky receded as a scroll when it is rolled up, and every mountain and island was moved out of its place" (Revelation 6:14).

This old world becomes very chaotic—a place where life is impossible. Whether radioactivity problems or major climate change, we can't know. For sure, it is going to be impossible to sustain life during that thousand-year period.

> "The kings of the earth, the great men, the rich men, the commanders, the mighty men, every slave and every free man, hid themselves in the caves and in the rocks of the mountains, and said to the mountains and rocks, "Fall on us and hide us from the face of Him who sits on the throne and from the wrath of the Lamb! For the great day of His wrath has come, and who is able to stand?" (Revelation 6:15-17)

A few years ago I conducted a Bible seminar in Colorado Springs, Colorado. The people who lived there told me about a nearby site back in the mountains where they have a presidential command post in case of atomic attack. In the day of Jesus' coming, the rocks and the mountains are not going to be enough to protect them.

> "I saw an angel standing in the sun; and he cried with a loud voice, saying to all the birds that fly in the midst of heaven, 'Come and gather together for the supper of the great God, that you may eat the flesh of kings, the flesh of captains, the flesh of mighty men, the flesh of horses and of those who sit on them, and the flesh of all people, free and slave, both small and great.'" (Revelation 19:17, 18)

All who are left on this earth, the Bible says, are going to be dead. We read another description in the book of Jeremiah: "At that day the slain of the Lord shall be from one end of the earth even to the other end of the earth. They shall not be lamented, or gathered, or buried; they shall become refuse on the ground" (Jeremiah 25:33).

They are not lamented because there is no one left to lament them. They're not gathered because there is no one left to gather them. This earth is going to be void, and that too takes place when Christ returns, even though He does not touch the ground. So what takes place during the thousand years? Revelation tells us again about Satan being bound with that chain.

"I saw an angel coming down from heaven, having the key to the bottomless pit and a great chain in his hand. He laid hold of the dragon, that serpent of old, who is the Devil and Satan, and bound him for a thousand years; and he cast him into the bottomless pit, and shut him up, and set a seal on him, so that he should deceive the nations no more till the thousand years were finished. But after these things he must be released for a little while." (Revelation 20:1-3)

I've heard people say that Satan would be bound with a chain of circumstances. In other words, there would be no one to tempt, so he's bound. There's no question that is true. There's also no question that he's going to be imprisoned as well. God is going to restrict him. This is the beginning of the end for Satan, and he is going to be restricted to this barren earth where he and his angels can see the result of their rebellion.

Jeremiah continues with a description of this earth during that time: "I beheld the earth, and indeed it was without form, and void; and the heavens, they had no light. I beheld the mountains, and indeed they trembled, and all the hills moved back and forth" (Jeremiah 4:23, 24).

This world will not be inhabited during this time. A prevalent teaching is that the Lord is going to come to earth and set up His kingdom—with people driving around in cars, and with smog, sin, sinners, and everything else—and He's going to give everyone a second chance. When He doesn't work it out with some of these people who keep being rebellious, He'll take them off somewhere and destroy them. But the picture in Scripture is the earth in destruction. The Bible says this earth is going to be without form and void—there is not going to be any light, and no one can even live when the world is in that condition. I believe it because the Bible says it.

"I beheld, and indeed there was no man, and all the birds of the heavens had fled. I beheld, and indeed the fruitful land was a wilderness, and all its cities were broken down at the presence of the Lord, by His fierce anger." (Jeremiah 4: 25, 26)

When you continue to get the same picture throughout Scripture, there can be no question about the condition of this world during that time.

"Behold, the Lord makes the earth empty and makes it waste, distorts its surface and scatters abroad its inhabitants. ... The land shall be entirely emptied and utterly plundered, for the Lord has spoken this word." (Isaiah 24:1, 3)

That's the picture during those thousand years. That's this earth—without form and void—and the wicked one, the devil, is bound. The saints are gone. They are in heaven, rejoicing, but they are also doing something else.

"I saw thrones, and they sat on them, and judgment was committed to them. Then I saw the souls of those who had been beheaded for their witness to Jesus and for the word of God, who had not worshiped the beast or his image, and had not received his mark on their foreheads or on their hands. And they lived and reigned with Christ for a thousand years." (Revelation 20:4)

Praise the Lord! Often, when people give their hearts and their lives to Jesus Christ, they will tell me, "I just don't know if I would have the courage to resist that pressure." Surely, you *would* trust in Jesus. He's the one who gives you the courage when it's needed. What could be more wonderful than to give your life for God if you had to do it? What could be greater? We live a whole life, and we don't always do much that is worthwhile, do we? Then to stand for truth, which is right—that would be great.

No true believer anywhere will not stand up and say, "Listen, I believe, and I'm going to stand for truth. I'm going to go where Jesus leads me, even if other people who claim to be believers are going another direction." How do I know that you will do and say this? It is because you are willing to do it right now. You're willing to stand up for Him and for truth right now—right now when no one has a gun to your head; right now when no one has a noose around your neck; right now when no one is trying to force you into anything, you have the courage to stand right now. You see, if we don't have the courage to stand today, if we won't do it now, we won't do it then, right?

Now is the day that we settle that. Now is the day that we make the decision that we will follow God's truth. As a result, God says, during the thousand years we are going to be judges.

"Do you not know that the saints will judge the world? And if the world will be judged by you, are you unworthy to judge the smallest matters? Do you not know that we shall judge angels? How much more, things that pertain to this life?" (1 Corinthians 6:2, 3)

I didn't say that—God says it. When does this judgment take place? It takes place during the thousand years. It takes a while to review this whole sin situation.

When a man receives Jesus Christ, his name is written in the book of life. Everyone whose name is in that book of life when Christ says that it's finished and we're going down to get them. Everyone is either dead and will come forth in the resurrection, or those who are alive will rise into the air from the earth. Everyone whose name is written in that book has been judged already and found righteous by the blood of Jesus, and they are saved.

Let's say you get to heaven and you look around and wonder, "Where is brother so-and-so? Where's doctor so-and-so? Where's pastor so-and-so? Where's old Joe? Why isn't he here?"

You could go through all of eternity with those questions on your mind. Why isn't my son here? Why isn't my daughter here? Why isn't my husband here? Why isn't my wife here? Why isn't anyone else I know here? You could go through eternity wondering about that, wondering too about the angels and what really happened to those angels—why they made the decisions they made. Why did Lucifer make the decision that he made?

During those thousand years, all questions are answered forever. God doesn't run some kind of hush-hush government. He doesn't run something off in a back room somewhere. It is all laid on the table. If you want to know why somebody isn't there, you'll be able to look. You'll see that they never really made a decision for Christ. That's it. When you make a decision for Christ, you'll follow through on the truths as you see them in God's Word. If you've made that commitment to Christ, you're not going to be tied down to what some relative says, what some friend says, what *anyone* says. You're simply going to say, "I want to follow Him and His truth because I love Him." So that's going to be the key.

This period of judgment takes place, and you are able to ask questions. All cases are reviewed, and you see that God is just. We look at God and see that He is just—He is just. We sometimes attribute things to God that are not just. God is *always* just.

We see first that Christ returns; second, the righteous are resurrected; third, the righteous are translated; fourth, the wicked are destroyed; and fifth, Satan is bound—we've seen this all predicted. The wicked are destroyed; they die—but that's not the second death, however. So what happens at the end of the thousand years? "But the rest of the dead did not live again until the thousand years were finished. This is the first resurrection" (Revelation 20:5).

If you look at the entire scripture, you see that the first resurrection takes place, "but the rest of the dead lived not again until the thousand years were finished"—and this is when the second resurrection takes place. So we see that in second resurrection, the wicked are raised.

They were destroyed by the brightness of Christ's coming, but a thousand years later, they are resurrected. Satan will seem to have a new power, and when he is loosed at this time for a little season, he will convince the wicked that he is the one who resurrected them. He will persuade them that he is the one who gave them life, and he will assure them that they are going to be victorious.

"Then I, John, saw the holy city, New Jerusalem, coming down out of heaven from God, prepared as a bride adorned for her husband" (Revelation 21:2). Christ will come and take the saints to heaven with Him for a thousand years. A judgment will take place during that thousand years, and we see that everything has been done according to how God would have it done—that His way is true; it is righteous; it is great.

Then there will be a special resurrection—the second resurrection of those who are wicked. The New Jerusalem will descend to earth. The wicked will look up and see it coming down. This is the bride; this is the city—it's not that dirty old place over there in the Holy Land. That place is going to be laid open—you can read of it in the Scriptures. The New Jerusalem is going to hover over a mountain and settle down on it. What an event that it will be. While the New Jerusalem is coming down, with all the saints in it, what does Satan do? "They went up on the breadth of the earth and surrounded the camp of the saints and the beloved city. And fire came down from God out of heaven and devoured them" (Revelation 20:9).

The wicked will surround the city, ready to destroy it, and they will think they are going to take it. You know, sometimes people say to me that if the wicked could have a second chance, they would accept. No, they don't—they prove that they would not. They're not going up to the city, saying, "Lord, we love You. We've made mistakes, so please forgive us, and take us back." They are not doing that. We're talking here about the "second-chance" theory.

For example, a lot of people today talk about another chance for the Jews. Listen, the Jews have had chance after chance, and the Jews are having another chance right now. Right now, the Jewish nation as a whole could say they are going to accept Jesus.

Individually, you will find many, many individual Jews who are accepting Christ—what a beautiful thing that is. More than 600,000 Messianic Jews are in America. Somebody says 600,000 is not very many, but that's a lot of Messianic Jews that are Jews by birth and are registered. I believe many millions of what I call "closet Christians" are Jews that really believe in Jesus. I believe that, but, my friend, the second chance, the third chance, the fourth chance, the fifth chance—we've all had many chances, haven't we?

This is the *last* chance. What will happen at the very end is proof that no matter how many chances they had, they will never worship God—they will come forth to try to destroy Him and to try to destroy the city, but the Bible says that fires comes down from God out of heaven and devours them. "The devil, who deceived them, was cast into the lake of fire and brimstone where the beast and the false prophet are. And they will be tormented day and night forever and ever" (Revelation 20:10).

The Bible says that this earth is going to be remade after those wicked are destroyed. This is why I believe that while that New Jerusalem is sitting right above this earth, before it actually touches the ground, we're going to see Creation again. Just as in the original first six days of Creation, we're going to see this earth completely remade—beautiful, totally whole, fantastic—and then the New Jerusalem is going to settle down on this earth. This is going to be our home, right here in the New Jerusalem with Christ throughout all eternity.

I hope that you are like that man in Philadelphia mentioned as this chapter began, who said, "Now it all fits together." There are always so many little missing pieces and ideas that just can't be found in the Bible.

God says that He will put an end to sin. He will take His saints to heaven for a thousand years, where with Him they will review—a judgment review—to see why some were not saved. Then the New Jerusalem will be brought to this earth. Satan will try to take it, and he and all the wicked will be destroyed. The Bible says that fire will come down from heaven; this earth will be rebuilt; and it literally will become heaven for us—this earth will become our home. Second Peter 3:10-13 reads:

> "The day of the Lord will come as a thief in the night, in which the heavens will pass away with a great noise, and the elements will melt with fervent heat; both the earth and the works that are in

it will be burned up. Therefore, since all these things will be dissolved, what manner of persons ought you to be in holy conduct and godliness, looking for and hastening the coming of the day of God, because of which the heavens will be dissolved, being on fire, and the elements will melt with fervent heat? Nevertheless we, according to His promise, look for new heavens and a new earth in which righteousness dwells."

Without destruction of the old heaven and earth, the new heaven and earth cannot be created. In that new earth will be the tree of life.

"In the middle of its street, and on either side of the river, was the tree of life, which bore twelve fruits, each tree yielding its fruit every month. The leaves of the tree were for the healing of the nations." (Revelation 22:2)

The tree of life will be restored to this earth because God said that it will be. Even though it was removed from this earth, the Bible says it is going to be restored at the end of the millennium.

"Now I saw a new heaven and a new earth, for the first heaven and the first earth had passed away. Also there was no more sea. Then I, John, saw the holy city, New Jerusalem, coming down out of heaven from God, prepared as a bride adorned for her husband. And I heard a loud voice from heaven saying, 'Behold, the tabernacle of God is with men, and He will dwell with them, and they shall be His people. God Himself will be with them and be their God.'" (Revelation 21:1-3)

The Bible tells us Jesus comes three times to this earth. He came first to live among us and to give His life for us on the cross. He is soon to return a second time to take His faithful ones home to heaven for a thousand years. Then, He returns to earth a third time to destroy sin and sinners and rebuild earth as our home with Him forever.

It's not hard to believe the book of Revelation if you simply read it and trust what God promises is going to take place. When you do, all the pieces come together—they make sense; they fit!

CHAPTER 11

God's Messages— God's Messengers

W e live at a time when everybody seems to be talking. Maybe not everybody is listening, but people definitely are talking! Cell phones seem permanently fixed to many human ears. And if not used for speaking, phones serve to send messages by "texting." E-mail has long since surpassed old-fashioned handwritten letters—and countless e-mails fly instantly from any point on earth to any other. Online, untold millions communicate with each other on social-networking sites or through instant-messaging services.

God, too, is a major Communicator. In fact, He invented communication. The Bible even calls Him "the Word."

In the beginning, before man sinned, God talked with man face to face, as a father would speak to his children. When the Lord desired to make known certain things to Adam and Eve in the Garden of Eden, He spoke to them close up and in person.

However, after man sinned, he could no longer bear to look upon the face of his God and live. You will recall that when Adam and Eve heard the voice of God, after they had disobeyed His commandments, they hid themselves behind the trees in the garden. Sin always separates man from God. Sin severed the direct connection—the direct line of face-to-face communication with God.

In order that people might still have instruction from heaven that God wished to give to them, God began to call certain people to do this work on His behalf, and He called them prophets. He revealed instructions to these prophets, and in turn, they communicated with God's true people. From generation to generation, God has called men and women to be His spokespeople.

- "God, who at various times and in various ways spoke in time past to the fathers by the prophets" (Hebrews 1:1).

- "Surely the Lord God does nothing, unless He reveals His secret to His servants the prophets" (Amos 3:7).

Let me illustrate this. If your telephone line was cut or your cell service went out, you could no longer talk to the person on the other end of the line. God loved us enough after sin entered the word that He called men and women, giving them the name of "prophet" or "prophetess," to reveal His messages to His people.

How does God reveal His will to prophets? In the Bible we are told of three principle ways He has used. The first is that He gave the prophets divine understanding and supernatural knowledge. He spoke to men "who had understanding of the times, to know what Israel ought to do" (1 Chronicles 12:32).

The second way God used to reveal His will to the prophets was by guiding their minds in their speaking and writing, so they spoke and wrote the truths God desired the people to have. In 2 Peter 1:21, we are told how we received our Bibles: "For prophecy never had its origin in the will of man, but men spoke from God as they were carried along by the Holy Spirit" (NIV). Also, David said: "The Spirit of the Lord spoke through me; his word was on my tongue" (2 Samuel 23:2).

The third way in which God revealed His will through the prophets was to give dreams and visions to them. "When a prophet of the Lord is among you, I reveal myself to him in visions, I speak to him in dreams" (Numbers 12:6 NIV).

I now raise a pertinent question. Has the Lord placed the gift of prophecy in the Christian church for our time today? Our answer is found in 1 Corinthians 12:28:

> "In the church God has appointed first of all apostles, second prophets, third teachers, then workers of miracles, also those having gifts of healing, those able to help others, those with gifts of administration, and those speaking in different kinds of tongues." (NIV)

God has placed the gift of the spirit of prophecy in His church. It is to continue down through all time.

Notice that the gift of prophecy is not the leading gift that God gave. It does not rank first. Some are inclined to put undue emphasis on the gift of prophecy. It does not rank first in the Bible, so we cannot place it first. Notice which gift does rank first: "God has appointed first of all apostles."

The word "apostles" cannot be restricted just to the twelve that Jesus chose. The Bible speaks of other men aside from the first twelve as also being apostles. Truly, John the Baptist was an apostle, for an apostle means one sent forth or one sent of God to preach the message of God. We could name some others in more recent times, such as Martin Luther and John Wesley.

In turning to 1 Corinthians 12, we notice that Paul compared the church to the human body. The various gifts of the Holy Ghost are likened to the various members of the body, such as the ear, the eye, mouth, hand, and the feet. What place does the spirit of prophecy or gift of prophecy hold in God's church? We find our answer in 1 Samuel 9:9: "Formerly in Israel, if a man went to inquire of God, he would say, 'Come, let us go to the seer,' because the prophet of today used to be called a seer" (NIV).

Notice the importance of the gift of the prophet in the church. The gift of prophecy is just as important to the church as the eye is to the body. So a church without this gift cannot see clearly and is at least partially blind. Bible prophecies, of course, still point the way ahead, but God's plan is to help His last-day followers "fill in the details" of those earlier prophecies, as they draw close to the time when those prophesied events are about to happen. Any new information that comes to us today through this gift will always harmonize completely with prophecies of long ago, of course. But God does want to share new information, so that the events of the near future are in sharp, detailed focus.

And a church without this gift also cannot see all the other truth God has for it. All the truth God shared with us in His Word is accurate and unchangeable. But again, for those of us living just before His return, He also has a "present truth" that applies far more to our own time than to any age in the past. This present truth will, of course, always harmonize with past truth, but it is a huge loss to us if we miss out on the truth God wants to share with His church today.

Now, how many of you have seen a counterfeit $13 bill? No one has. Why? You answer truly that you cannot have a counterfeit or false unless there is a genuine. Here then, when Jesus spoke of when in the last days of time we should beware of false prophets, He shows that true prophets will also exist then.

The next question to answer is this: "Did all of the prophets of Bible times write a book of the Bible?" Acts 11:27, 28 speaks of a prophet called

Agabus. Though he was a prophet, we have no book of the Bible with his name. In Acts 13:1, Simon and Barnabas are spoken of, but again, we find no books of the Bible written by them. In Acts 15:32, we read of two other prophets whose names were Silas and Judas; yet, they did not write a book of the Bible.

Not only did God call men to be prophets, but He also called women to be prophetesses. Some people are especially opposed to a religion where a woman takes any leading part. They lay special stress on a text Paul wrote: "Women should remain silent in the churches. They are not allowed to speak, but must be in submission, as the Law says" (1 Corinthians 14:34 NIV).

Some want the men to do all the preaching. Yet, if you will notice this chapter carefully, you will discover that Paul is speaking about those who were carried away emotionally with false tongues or languages. Paul said for them to keep silence in the church.

The best answer to this above statement is that the Almighty God, in the time covered by the Bible, called nine different women to be prophetesses. In Luke 2:36, we are told about one called Anna. Judges 4:4 speaks about Deborah, a prophetess and a judge of Israel. You will find that whenever God could not find a willing man to do the work, He called a woman to do it.

In Exodus 15:20, we read of the sister of Moses, Miriam, who was a prophetess. Also in Nehemiah 6:14, Noadiah is mentioned as a prophetess. Second Kings 22:14 speaks of Huldah as having the prophetic gift. Then, in Acts 21:9, we notice that Philip, one of the seven deacons, had four daughters who were prophetesses. We need not be surprised then, if in the last days God would call a woman to be His messenger.

Again, I ask the question: "How long is the prophetic gift to be in the church?" Ephesians gives us a full answer. "When He ascended on high, He led captivity captive, and gave gifts to men" (Ephesians 4:8).

How did He lead captivity captive? According to Matthew 27:52, when Christ left this world, He took with Him a sample of the race He died to redeem—those who were resurrected with Him. What were these gifts spoken of that He gave unto men? "He Himself gave some to be apostles, some prophets, some evangelists, and some pastors and teachers" (Ephesians 4:11).

These, then, were the gifts He gave after His resurrection. Notice these gifts again: apostles, prophets, evangelists, pastors, and teachers. Why were they given? They were furnished "for the equipping of the saints for the work of ministry, for the edifying of the body of Christ" (Ephesians 4:12).

How long were they to be in the church? "Till we all come to the unity of the faith and of the knowledge of the Son of God, to a perfect man, to the measure of the stature of the fullness of Christ" (Ephesians 4:13).

Would you answer a question for me? When will it be that we will all be in a unity of the faith and of the knowledge of the Son of God and be perfect men and women? The answer is obvious, isn't it? We won't be in the unity of the faith until the end of time. Jesus, here, is simply stating that the gift of prophecy will go on until He comes again, for we will never come into the full stature of Jesus Christ until He comes again. Then we shall be like Him, for we shall see Him as He is. So, according to the Scriptures, apostles, prophets, evangelists, pastors, and teachers are to be with us in the church until the end of time.

For many centuries, Christians looked around and saw little evidence that the gift of prophecy was still at work in God's church. Most decided that the gift had ceased with the passing of the apostles. But they had overlooked the words of the prophet Joel. In talking about the last days—the time just before Christ's second coming—Joel said this:

"It shall come to pass afterward that I will pour out My Spirit on all flesh; your sons and your daughters shall prophesy, your old men shall dream dreams, your young men shall see visions. And also on My menservants and on My maidservants I will pour out My Spirit in those days." (Joel 2:28, 29)

This prophecy applies to our time—today—right here in the early years of this new millennium. Did you notice that these verses make clear that both "sons" and "daughters" will prophesy in our time?

It's wonderful that God wants to speak to us through this great gift, but it also means we have to be on guard. Because the devil always—*always*—counterfeits any good gift God gives us, we can expect false prophets and a false gift of prophecy to show up and be seen right alongside the genuine.

All any of us needs to do is just look around, and we find people claiming to be prophets—to be able to predict the future and speak for God. But beware. Many of these are false prophets. And the *only* way to know the difference between them is to carefully study the Bible. God's Word offers tests we can use to know the false from the true. For example:

- Fulfilled prophecies: Deuteronomy 18:22; Jeremiah 28:8, 9.

- Harmony with the Bible: Isaiah 8:20.

- The fruit of the prophet's life and work: Matthew 7:16-20.

- A true prophet doesn't add a private interpretation: 2 Peter 1:20.

Countless Christians today are being deceived and misled by those claiming to be God's prophets—but who in reality are on the devil's payroll. Still, the very existence of a counterfeit means there's a genuine to be found, and indeed, there is.

Did the Bible's prediction that the gift of prophecy would be with us to the end of time come to pass? Has that gift been present even in these years as we wait for the return of Jesus? Let me tell you now of something that happened back in the mid-1800s—something few know about.

Around that time in the mid-1800s, a young girl 17 years of age by the name of Ellen G. Harmon was living in Portland, Maine. She was given a vision and told to go to Poland, Maine, and to tell the people of the vision that the Lord had given her. She was ill with tuberculosis. The doctor said one lung was completely gone and that the other was badly affected. Hemorrhages from the lungs had reduced her, until she weighed about 70 pounds. It looked as if she would live but a few weeks. She had been confined to her bed.

She called her brother to her bedside and said, "I want you to arrange for a carriage, for we must go to Poland to tell the people what the Lord has shown me." He remonstrated with her and said, "Sister, you are too weak. How can you go and address a crowd of people? Look how you've coughed, and you've been hemorrhaging." But realizing that she would not take no for an answer—for she assured him that "the One who told me to go will give me the strength to do it"—he consented and secured a carriage and took her there.

The believers were assembled. She told those people the vision and gave some messages of reproof to certain people the Lord had revealed to her. Ellen Harmon, instead of dying as the doctors had predicted, lived on for 71 more years. Think of it! She was wonderfully used of God.

In August of 1846, she married James White, an Adventist minister. Her name then became Mrs. E. G. White. She became the greatest religious writer of modern times. If you were to stack the different books that she wrote about the Bible, they would make a stack six feet tall. In the vaults in Washington, D. C. where her writings are kept, a total of a thousand of her personal letters and 47,000 pages of manuscripts that the Lord inspired her to write can be found there.

Some of these books comprise the "Conflict of the Ages" series, which traces the great conflict between truth and error from the fall of man in the Garden of Eden to Eden restored in the earth made new. There are five books in this series: *Patriarchs and Prophets, Prophets and Kings, The Desire of Ages, The Acts of the Apostles,* and *The Great Controversy.*

Besides these, she wrote many other books, one of which is *The Ministry of Healing.* She was neither a doctor nor a nurse, but this book is one of the best expositions on the principles of health and healing that the world has ever known. She called cancer a germ. Doctors made light of it in her day, but today many of them believe that cancer is a virus. She also stated that a vegetarian diet was the best. This also was laughed at and mocked as it was in her day; they said there could not possibly be a balance of protein without the eating of meat. Today, doctors again have assured the public that a vegetarian diet is the best diet. In her day, they believed that the night air was harmful, but she said that the windows should be opened at night to let in fresh air. Today, we all know the value of getting fresh air when we sleep. She also said that whole wheat bread was the best bread for family consumption. Again, this has been proven true, though in her day white bread was more commonly used.

She has written a number of other books. One called *Christ's Object Lessons* is recognized as the best exposition on the parables of Jesus. *The Desire of Ages,* according to one of the librarians at the Library of Congress, is the best book outside of the Bible on the life of Christ. She wrote a little volume on the Christian life called *Steps to Christ.* In this book is found a little sample of the Spirit of Prophecy. I hope that each one of you will read it if you haven't yet, and then let the Lord help you draw your own conclusions as to whether this woman was inspired or not. I know that after you read this book, you will know that God inspired her to write her many books.

The next questions we ask are: "What relationship do the writings of Mrs. Ellen G. White have with the Bible? Are they a part of the Bible?"

On several occasions, I have had the privilege of driving near Mt. Palomar in California. On top of Mt. Palomar is a large 200-inch telescope. I then ask, "As you look through that mirror, which in turn is focused on the heavens, and you see the many thousands of stars and galaxies there revealed—so many that it is impossible to see them with the naked eye—how many of these stars and galaxies did this telescope create?" The answer is: "It didn't create any of them. It only magnifies and reveals what God created so many years ago."

The same is true of the Spirit of Prophecy. As I read it, I find that it magnifies the Scriptures. It magnifies the true Word of God. In no way does it add to or subtract from the Word, but as a telescope, it only magnifies, and as a microscope, it brings out the detail. This is why the Spirit of Prophecy is so important and why so many people in God's remnant church avoid so many problems and are a happy people.

Every biblical test that can be brought to bear on the work and writings of Mrs. E. G. White proves that she had the gift of prophecy, and in no way are her books an addition to or a subtraction from the Bible.

The Spirit of Prophecy should never be used to prove Scripture, but Scripture should prove the Spirit of Prophecy. All of our doctrines should be taken from the Bible and the Bible alone. The doctrines of a Christian church should always without exception set forth the great divine standard, the Holy Scriptures. The Spirit of Prophecy will always draw you back to the study of God's Word.

I have read many books written by supposed prophets or men of God, but as I began to read them, I discovered that rather than leading me to the Bible, they convey other ideas and try to teach a new message. This never happens with the writings of Mrs. E. G. White. Every time I read any of her writings, it isn't long before I'm back reading the Bible, digging deeper into the Word as they reveal the deeper things of God.

Someone else says: "I notice that it says, according to Ephesians the fourth chapter, the Spirit of Prophecy was going to be given until we all come into the unity of the faith. Are there other churches that keep the seventh-day Sabbath?" Yes, there are. I know of a total of 53 churches that advocate the keeping of the seventh-day Sabbath. Most of them are local, one-church congregations. Notice why the spirit of prophecy was given:

"Till we all come to the unity of the faith and of the knowledge of the Son of God, to a perfect man, to the measure of the stature of the fullness of Christ; that we should no longer be children, tossed to and fro and carried about with every wind of doctrine, by the trickery of men, in the cunning craftiness of deceitful plotting." (Ephesians 4:13, 14)

The spirit of prophecy was given to unite us in a perfect message, a united message, one that will be the same the world around.

Satan has his counterpart of God's truth. The beast power is worldwide, but thank God that our Lord's message is worldwide, and this has largely been made possible by the work of the Spirit of Prophecy.

God used the Spirit of Prophecy to keep His church united during times of division and crisis, such as at the time of the Civil War. And from that time onward, through the servant of the Lord, Seventh-day Adventists have gone on to establish printing presses, hospitals, sanitariums, and institutions of learning all around the world, so we can say that God has truly used the Spirit of Prophecy.

The church's system of Christian education—which never could have been set up without this prophetic gift—is today one of the most far-reaching in all the world. Elementary, secondary, and college-university education is available world-wide. And students graduate from church colleges at three times the national percentage rate.

When Mrs. Ellen G. White passed to her rest in 1915, the *New York Independence*, a newspaper, wrote, "Whether she was a prophet or not, is not for us to say, but that she lived the life of a prophet and did the work of a prophet, no one can deny." Even the world, in this case, a worldly newspaper, recognized her as a prophetess of God.

It makes me happy that I am able to present to you such a wonderful truth as this. I cannot ask, "Do you accept all of the writings of Mrs. E. G. White?"—unless, of course, you have read them all. It would be impossible for you to pass judgment. So I invite you to read some of what she's written, and let God speak to your mind and heart about what you discover in the midst of her words.

Yes, God began communicating with His created human beings right there in the Garden of Eden—and He still has much to tell us today. One of His most important ways of reaching us is through the gift of prophecy.

Joel said the gift would be with us again near the end of history here on earth. He said not just men but women would exercise it. If God has something to tell me, I'm all ears—how about you? If He wants to preview the future between now and His soon return, I want to know what He's eager to share with me. If He has messages that tell me about my own life's purpose and His will for my being here, I want to know.

Every day, I'm bombarded with messages from all sides, but for sure, I don't want to miss any messages from God. I don't want to be so doubting and suspicious and skeptical about His promised gift of prophecy that I miss those vital messages.

So with an *open heart* to the Spirit's leading—and an *open Bible* to know what's true—and *open ears* to hear God speaking, I'll joyfully welcome His prophetic messages, custom-tailored just for me.

CHAPTER 12

Final Warning

This chapter is about serious stuff. If a warning says a massive hurricane is headed straight your way, then if at all possible, you get out of there. If a different warning says an escaped convict or a dangerous wild animal is on the loose, you pay attention. The Bible has issued a warning for everyone on earth—for here, and for now, and we are well advised to hear and act on it.

When I received the dream of building a television network that would reach the world with the three angels' messages of the Bible's book of Revelation, it was made clear to me that these warnings were to be the *undiluted three angels' messages—true messages to counteract the counterfeit.* For me not to give the direct message that Revelation 14 dictates would be a violation of that mandate from the Lord.

Do I enjoy giving a message of warning from Scripture and showing how the interpretation of that message is so clear that any honest seeker can see it? Of course not! I would rather preach the message of the cross and the love of God. But wait a minute. Who is giving this message in Revelation? It was Jesus Christ Himself who gave this message through the apostle John, who was known as the apostle of love. The revelation of, or about, Jesus Christ is what the book of Revelation contains. It is Christ's love letter to you and to me.

I don't know about you, but my parents often gave me stern warnings of things I should avoid. If you have children and you love them, you warn them of pitfalls they should avoid. Because He loves us, Jesus warns us through the third of the three angels of something that those living just before He returns will face. So, fasten your seat belt.

"Then a third angel followed them, saying with a loud voice, 'If anyone worships the beast and his image, and receives his mark on

his forehead or on his hand, he himself shall also drink of the wine
of the wrath of God, which is poured out full strength into the cup
of His indignation. He shall be tormented with fire and brimstone
in the presence of the holy angels and in the presence of the Lamb.' "
(Revelation 14:9, 10)

A beast, an image of that beast, and a mark—we'll discuss more on those
soon. First, though, we find in Revelation 13 that if you do not receive the
mark, there will be consequences:

"He causes all, both small and great, rich and poor, free and slave,
to receive a mark on their right hand or on their foreheads, and that
no one may buy or sell except one who has the mark or the name of
the beast, or the number of his name." (Revelation 13:16, 17)

Do you begin to see the significance of our study? God says a time is
coming when a boycott will be declared against those who do not have
this identifying characteristic, but that those who do receive it—whatever
it is—are going to incur the wrath of God. I think, having read these two
statements, we may begin to see the tremendous significance of this study.
This is a life-and-death matter, and no one knows it better than the devil.

One of the most solemn warnings anywhere in the pages of Scripture
is right here in the book of Revelation. I want you to notice that some do
heed the message as they are described in Revelation: "Here is the patience
of the saints; here are those who keep the commandments of God and the
faith of Jesus" (Revelation 14:12).

Notice that this same chapter goes on to describe the second coming
of Christ:

"I looked, and behold, a white cloud, and on the cloud sat One like
the Son of Man, having on His head a golden crown, and in His
hand a sharp sickle. And another angel came out of the temple,
crying with a loud voice to Him who sat on the cloud, 'Thrust in
Your sickle and reap, for the time has come for You to reap, for the
harvest of the earth is ripe.' " (Revelation 14:14, 15)

Jesus said that the harvest is "the end of the world." This, then, is God's
last warning message to be given to the world just before Christ returns.

Notice that Revelation 14:9 said, "If anyone," so it concerns us all.
Whatever that mark is, each of us knows that we don't want to receive it and

thereby incur the wrath of God. This message is in the heart of the book of Revelation. Some would like to have us believe that the book of Revelation is a closed book, but the very title means "reveal." Nothing can be revealed that is closed.

It is true that Revelation is a book full of symbolism. Why? I am sure I don't know all of God's mind in this regard, but I can think of at least a couple of good reasons. The first of them is that God is "cartooning" here, if you please, just a few broad strokes of history. Second, we discover that by using symbols, God has been able to veil some of these great truths from its enemies who would have destroyed the Book long before this. We wish to discover, then, using these symbols, what God's truth is for this time just before the second coming of Christ.

In order to escape the mark of the beast, we must know what is represented by this symbol of the beast. Also, we need to know who or what this beast power is.

"Then I stood on the sand of the sea. And I saw a beast rising up out of the sea, having seven heads and ten horns, and on his horns ten crowns, and on his heads a blasphemous name. Now the beast which I saw was like a leopard, his feet were like the feet of a bear, and his mouth like the mouth of a lion. The dragon gave him his power, his throne, and great authority." (Revelation 13:1, 2)

This must have been quite a sight to the apostle John, and I am sure it made quite an impression on him as he saw this beast rise up from the sea. It is the mark of this beast that you and I are to shun.

May I suggest right here in our study that when the Bible uses the term "beast," it is neither talking about some beastly doctrine, nor is not talking about some great heresy. What does a beast represent in Bible prophecy? The term "beast," as it is used in Bible prophecy, is not a disrespectful term. This is simply the term the Bible uses to represent a kingdom or nation as a political power.

We do the same thing today, don't we? If you see a cartoon with the picture of an eagle, you immediately know that the cartoonist is seeking to represent what nation? That represents the United States. If you see a bear, what do you know? That it represents Russia. Every so often, we have political conventions, and you see a donkey and an elephant. We use the same kind of thing today. God uses these cartoons, if you please—these symbols—to represent truths.

Notice a similar prophecy to the one we're studying in Revelation, and it is found in the book of Daniel. The Bible explains itself in a parallel prophecy, with no need for us to misunderstand. Daniel had seen a vision somewhat similar to John's. He saw a whole herd of animals coming up out of the sea: "Those great beasts, which are four, are four kings which arise out of the earth." He continued, "The fourth beast shall be a fourth kingdom on earth" (Daniel 7:17, 23).

All right, we have our key to understanding this prophecy. God said that in Bible prophecy, when an animal is used it is His method of representing some nation, some political power, in the world. Let us remember that it isn't necessarily a disrespectful term, but rather, the description of the beast will determine whether it is on the side of truth or on the side of error. Revelation 13 speaks of a beast with a mark. What is the mark? Who and what is that beast power? Let us take a further look at chapter 13 to see.

I believe the first identifying phrase is in the last part of verse 2: "The dragon gave him his power, his throne, and great authority" (Revelation 13:2).

Here we have a clue because we discover that this power gets its authority from the dragon, but what if we don't know who the dragon is? Ah, here again, the Bible is so clear in explaining itself. In Revelation we find a description of the dragon: "His tail drew a third of the stars of heaven and threw them to the earth. And the dragon stood before the woman who was ready to give birth, to devour her Child as soon as it was born" (Revelation 12:4).

Primarily, the dragon represents Satan. But the Bible goes on to leave no doubt: "So the great dragon was cast out, that serpent of old, called the Devil and Satan, who deceives the whole world; he was cast to the earth, and his angels were cast out with him" (Revelation 12:9).

Additionally, the devil always works through an earthly power. He doesn't walk down the street with horns and a long tail, carrying a pitchfork in his hand and with fire coming out of his ears. He works through some earthly power. What power was it that represented Satan standing before the woman (God's true people—Jeremiah 6:2; 2 Corinthians 11:2; Ephesians 5:23-27), ready to destroy Christ when He was born? Old pagan Rome under the Caesars was in power at the time of Christ. Herod, the Roman governor, declared that all Jewish male babies under two years of age should be killed. This is why Joseph and Mary fled to Egypt, as you may recall. The dragon, then, was the devil working through the old pagan Roman Empire—that is clear.

The dragon, you remember, was to give its power, seat of government, and authority to this beast power about whom we are concerned. Let me ask you this: "To what earthly power did pagan Rome give its seat of government and great authority?" I want to read a statement from a Roman Catholic historian:

> "When the Western empire fell into the hands of the barbarians, the Roman bishop was the only surviving heir of this imperial past, or, in the well-known dictum of Hobbes, 'the ghost of the deceased Roman empire sitting crowned upon the grave thereof.'"[1]

Notice another statement by a professor of history at the University of Rome: "To the succession of the Caesars came the succession of the pontiffs in Rome. When Constantine left Rome, he gave his seat to the pontiffs."[2] I think it is more than accidental that a Roman historian, in commenting on this very transaction of which we have spoken here, should use almost the same words the Bible used in prophesying the event that was to take place. We have only one clue so far that we have nailed down, and we certainly must be careful that we do not jump to conclusions. However, it is indisputable that Constantine surrendered his capital city, Rome, to the Roman Church—to Sylvester I, Bishop of Rome. That little religious-political power, no larger than a nine-hole golf course, wields a tremendous influence in this earth's politics.

We must examine more of these characteristics, because we dare not jump to conclusions. In the book of Revelation we discover that it is to be a religious power with some interesting characteristics. "They worshiped the dragon who gave authority to the beast; and they worshiped the beast, saying, 'Who is like the beast? Who is able to make war with him?' And he was given a mouth speaking great things and blasphemies'" (Revelation 13:4, 5).

I must ask this question at this point in our study. What is "blasphemy"? You have always heard that taking the Lord's name in vain is blasphemy, and indeed it is, but let us again turn to Scripture and let the Bible explain for us what its definition of blasphemy is. Here is an incident from the life of our Lord: "And the scribes and the Pharisees began to reason, saying, 'Who is this who speaks blasphemies? Who can forgive sins but God alone?'" (Luke 5:21).

Jesus had just forgiven a man of his sins, and here, we are told that blasphemy consists of the claim to forgive sin. Jesus had that power because

---

1   Philip Schaff, *History of the Christian Church*, Vol. 3, 5th edition (New York: Scribner, 1902), 287.

2   Mark Finley, *The Next Superpower: "Ancient Prophecies, Global Events, and Your Future* (Hagerstown MD: Review and Herald Publishing Association, 2005) 147.

He was God, but no man has it. The Bible also says that one of the characteristics of this power was to claim to have the power to forgive men's sins. Is that claim made by the church which, we have begun to see, would fit the description in this prophecy?

In the little book *The Dignity and Duties of the Priest*[3] is this startling statement: "The priest holds the place of the Saviour Himself, when by saying 'Ego te absolvo,' he absolves from sin. This great power, which Jesus Christ has received from His eternal Father, He has communicated to His priest."

Then the author of this manual for priests goes on to say that if Christ and the priest were to sit down together in confessional booths, side by side, and Christ should say, "*Ego te absolvo,*" and the priest should say, "*Ego te absolvo,*" the two penitents are equally absolved of their sins. Even though we are not sitting in judgment, we have simply read some identifying characteristics from Scripture, and then we ask, "Is there a power anywhere in the world that measures up to these identifying marks?" I believe we shall discover, as we continue to marshal the evidence, that it is not going to leave us to wonder as to the truth of what we are discovering.

I want to say right here, before we go further in our study, that I have some very wonderful Roman Catholic friends. It is not our intent here to be unkind or to throw stones. Yet, this is a message that concerns Jesus Christ, and it concerns your destiny and mine, and we can do nothing else than open it and say, "If it is the truth, I want to know. Lord, speak to us."

The Bible tells us a little more about this matter of blasphemy in another incident from the life of our Lord: "The Jews answered Him, saying, 'For a good work we do not stone You, but for blasphemy, and because You, being a Man, make Yourself God'" (John 10:33).

Here is another aspect of the definition of blasphemy as being when one claims to take the place of God. Is this claim, made by the power that we have discovered here, beginning to fit closely the description in Revelation 13? I would like to read again from this same manual for priests. Pope Innocent III has written: "Indeed, it is not too much to say that in view of the sublimity of their offices, the priests are so many gods."[4]

Please realize that I did not say these words; I merely quoted them. Notice that we are not reading from the critics of the Roman Catholic Church—we are reading from their own sources, and I don't know how else to be fair and intellectually honest as we approach this subject. Here are a couple of

3   St. Alphonsus de Liguori, *Dignity and Duties of the Priest* (New York, Cincinnati, Chicago: Genziger Brothers, 1889), 34.

4   *Ibid.,* 36.

other statements I want to share with you. The following is from an article on the pope (this is not some critic writing in disgust—this is a Roman Catholic author): "The pope is of so great dignity and so exalted that he's not a mere man, but, as it were, God, and the vicar of God. He is likewise the divine monarch and supreme emperor and king of kings."[5] "So that if it were possible that the angels might err in the faith, they could be judged and excommunicated by the pope.[6]

Consider too these words: "We hold upon this earth the place of God almighty."[7] I think we need have no question here in our minds. These quotations from the Roman Catholics' own writings place the papacy squarely under the searchlight of this prophecy.

God did not want us to err or go astray in our understanding here. He gave us some mathematical proof. Mathematics, you know, is the only exact science. God had put within the heart of this prophecy mathematical proof, so that we need not misunderstand.

"And he was given a mouth speaking great things and blasphemies, and he was given authority to continue for forty-two months. Then he opened his mouth in blasphemy against God, to blaspheme His name, His tabernacle, and those who dwell in heaven. It was granted to him to make war with the saints and to overcome them. And authority was given him over every tribe, tongue, and nation." (Revelation 13:5-7)

Forty-two months—in Bible prophecy God used a scale in which a day is used to represent a year. In Numbers 14:34 and Ezekiel 4:6 we find that principle, and Bible scholars have used this key for centuries. Forty-two months would represent how many days? Forty-two months multiplied by thirty days (the Jewish calendar allows for just 30 days per month) equals 1,260 days. Our key said that a day represents a year. Then this apostate power was to exercise authority and make war with the saints for 1,260 years.

5   Lucius Ferraris, *Prompta Bibliotheca Canonica, Juridica, Moralis, Theologica, Ascetica, Polemica, Rubristica, Historica,* Volume VI (Paris: J. P. Migne, 1852), 25.

6   Uriah Smith, *The Prophecies of Daniel and the Revelation* (Whitefish, Montana: Kessinger Publishing, LLC, 2004), 129.

7   Pope Leo XIII, "The Reunion of Christendom," Encyclical Letter, June 20, 1894, as translated in *The Great Encyclical Letters of Pope Leo XIII* (New York: Benziger, 1903) 304.

In the year A.D. 538, the Roman Church had become supreme in the world. In A.D. 538, the last opposition of the surrounding nations finally crumbled, and the Roman Church sat crowned upon the throne of the world. If we add to that the length of time this power was to continue (538 + 1,260) we arrive at the year 1798.

In the year 1797, Napoleon sent his armies into Rome. He told them to take the pope prisoner and transport him back to France, but they returned with nothing. Why? There was no reason that any astute military man could think of as to why the French armies did not go in and take the pope captive, but I will tell you why. The clock of God's prophecy had not yet struck the hour.

In 1798, the very next year, Napoleon sent General Berthier into the city of Rome, and just as the clock of prophecy struck the hour, Berthier took the pope captive, took a whole load of priceless treasures from the Vatican back to France, and the Vatican as a world power virtually ceased to exist. Do the math, as they say: A.D. 538–A.D. 1798 is 1,260 years. Can there be any question?

"And I saw one of his heads as if it had been mortally wounded, and his deadly wound was healed. And all the world marveled and followed the beast" (Revelation 13:3). So, you see the extension of this prophecy. There was to be a mortal wound, yet that wound would be healed, and that power, of which we are speaking, was to be restored again to world prominence.

Have you noticed the resurgence of this power in the world today? It was in 1929 that the pope signed a concordat with Mussolini, restoring full power and independent rule to Vatican City again. Associated Press news releases at the time carried the statement—"The wound that has festered for so many years has been healed"[8]—the very terminology of the Bible!

But even more recent than that, notice how amazingly this prophecy is being fulfilled! Not so many years ago Pope Paul VI stood as the very ambassador of peace in the United Nations. After returning to Vatican City, he stood before the second Vatican Council, then in session, and said, "All the world was watching." You know how true that was. The prophecy said, "All the world wondered after the beast." The deadly wound would be healed—no longer was it a power to be trodden underfoot, but rather, all the world would stand in awe of it. His statement then, was nothing to the impact that a live appearance of the Pope brings today. No athletic event or concert by an entertainer will come close to matching it for live attendance and media coverage world wide.

---

8   Associate Press, *San Francisco Chronicle*, February 12, 1929, page 1.

Do you know that when Adventists began preaching this message more than a century ago, we preached it by faith? The only thing we could say was, "It is going to come about. There is going to come a time when the people of the earth are going to look upon the Roman Church, not with the animosity that they do now, but with great feelings of brotherly love and compassion. There will be attempts to unite, to merge the Christian churches, including the Catholic." I say, we preached it by faith then. We don't have to preach it by faith anymore because we see it being fulfilled today in our newspapers. What a day to be alive!

We have discovered that this power was to be pagan Rome's successor. There was no other. We have discovered that it was to be a power speaking great blasphemy. It filled that qualification. Persecuting the saints of the most high, it said. Careful and conservative historians tell us that during the period called the Dark Ages more than 50 million people were put to death because they would not accept the state church. We have discovered that it was dominant in world affairs for 1,260 years—that it would be wounded and then revived.

We have only one more clue to examine, and then I think we will have incontrovertibly established the identity of this power in Revelation 13:18: "Here is wisdom. Let him who has understanding calculate the number of the beast, for it is the number of a man: His number is 666."

What can this mean? This number, 666, must have some significance in connection with the title or authority of the person at the head of this organization, represented here by the beast power. Here is an interesting statement from a weekly Catholic newspaper. A number of years ago it stated in its "Question Box" section:

> "*Is it true that the words of the Apocalypse in the 13th chapter, 18th verse refer to the Pope? ... The words referred to here: "Here is wisdom. He that hath understanding, let him count the number of the beast. For it is the number of a man; and the number of him is six hundred sixty-six." The title of the Pope of Rome is Vicarius Filii Dei — if you take the letters of his title which represent Latin numerals and add them together they come to 666.*"[9]

---

9 "Question Box," *Our Sunday Visitor*, November 15, 1914. NOTE: This same question and answer appeared twice in the Catholic newspaper *Our Sunday Visitor*, but in fairness to the writer, some years later he printed a retraction.

"However, this is one of the leading titles that is given to the Pope, Vicar of the Son of God in English and Vicarius Filii Dei in Latin. ... Now if this were the only identifying characteristic, it would mean nothing. There are many names that when you apply this method can be made to come out with the number 666. But how many are world wide powers? Powers which came up after pagan Rome had gone down, built itself up in the city of Rome, was a religious power, claimed the authority to forgive sins, took the very titles of Deity, and ruled for 1260 years? What power except the papacy ever did all of that? None."[10]

No question can remain in anyone's mind that in the entire world no other power fits these qualifications. If this is so, then this power spoken of in Revelation 13 is the great papal power. The thing we want to know next is: "What is the mark?"

For just a moment, we must go back to the days of the Reformation, to the time of Martin Luther, John Calvin, John Knox, John Wesley, and the other great men who followed in their wake. We discovered a few moments ago that the mark of the beast was to be a message presented immediately before the second coming of Christ; therefore, it was not an issue in the time of Martin Luther or Knox and Huss and these others.

The issue was this: Luther said that the Bible and the Bible only ought to be the Christian's rule of faith and practice. Do you remember from history the dialogue between Luther and one of the vicars, who asked what would happen if the Bible was available to every pot boy and swineherd? Luther replied, "We would have more Christians, Father." Luther believed that the Bible ought to be the sole source of authority for every Christian. This was the bombshell that nearly shook the papacy apart. Luther saw nothing of relics, images, and penance when he got hold of a Bible (by the way, he was a priest before he ever read one), but he saw much of righteousness by faith. Remember those words, "The just shall live by faith *alone?*"

Luther shocked the papacy by stipulating "the Bible and the Bible only" is the rule of faith and practice for the Christian. Except for the man Ignatius Loyola, the papacy might have succumbed to the onslaught of the Reformation. He studied into reestablishing the Church of Rome in its relationship to the new Protestant threat. The Council of Trent was called, which lasted for eighteen years. The purpose of this council was to study how the church might combat the threat of Protestantism. The question was, "Can

---

10   H.M.S. Richards, *What Jesus Said* (Nashville, TN: Southern Publishing Association, 1957) 467.

the church weather the storm? Does it have an answer to this threat?" *The Schaff-Herzog Encyclopedia* says this, in its article entitled, "The Council of Trent": "From a doctrinal and disciplinary point of view, it was the most important council in the history of the Roman Church, fixing her distinctive faith and practice in relation to the Protestant evangelical churches."[11]

The council debated for years and finally settled on a way the Catholic Church might successfully refute the arguments presented by the Protestant theologians. Do you know what their argument was? The argument that stopped the Reformation was this: "Tradition, not Scripture, is the foundation of the Catholic church." This statement comes from a Catholic theologian by the name of Nampon in his book *Catholic Doctrine as Defined by the Council of Trent*:[12] "Tradition, not Scripture, is the rock upon which the church of Jesus Christ is built."

The question that remains is: "How could they ever have sold this idea to the rest of the world?" Do you want me to tell you what carried the day? Do you know what carried the argument and made it absolutely watertight? This is a statement by Dr. H. J. Holzman, in his book, *Canon and Tradition*:[13]

"Finally, at the last opening [of the Council of Trent], on the 18th of January 1563, their last scruple was laid aside. The Archbishop of Reggio made a speech in which he openly declared that tradition stood above the Scriptures. The authority of the church could no longer be bound by the authority of the Scriptures because the church had changed the Sabbath into Sunday, not by the command of Christ, but by its own authority."

Do you see? This is the reason they could say that tradition takes the place of Scripture. The reason they knew it did was that while there was nothing in the Scripture about Sundays replacing the seventh day of the week as a day of worship, the whole Christian world was worshiping on Sunday because the Catholic Church had made the change! Do you see why it was such a foolproof argument? Do you see why the Protestants could not argue with

11   Reverend Philip Schaff, Johann Jakob Herzog, *Encyclopedia of Religious Knowledge,* (London: Funk & Wagnalls Company, 1914).

12   Rev. A. Nampon, S.J., *Catholic Doctrine as Defined by the Council of Trent* (Philadelphia: Peter F. Cunningham & Son, 1869) 40.

13   Heinrich Julius Holtzmann, *Canon and Tradition* (Ludwigsburg: Druck and Verlag von Ferd. Riehm, 1859), 263.

them? It was because *they too* had accepted the first day of the week as a day of worship. That argument carried the day.

The Bible predicted in the parallel Old Testament passage (Daniel 7:25) that a power would arise that would think to change God's law. That is just exactly what happened. Have they done it? Have they sought to make that change? They make no apology, and if you have studied Catholic doctrine, you know that it is true.

Here is a statement by Rev. Peter Geiermann, C.S.S.R., in his famous book, *The Convert's Catechism of Catholic Doctrine:*[14]

Q. What is the Third Commandment?

A. The Third Commandment is: Remember that thou keep holy the Sabbath day.

Q. Which is the Sabbath day?

A. Saturday is the Sabbath day.

Q. Why do we observe Sunday instead of Saturday?

A. We observe Sunday instead of Saturday because the Catholic Church transferred the solemnity from Saturday to Sunday.

Here, a Catholic author says that the third commandment (and you know that they have omitted the second so the fourth commandment in our Bibles is referred to as the third commandment in the Catholic Catechism) commands men to worship God in a special manner on Sunday, the Lord's day. No wonder, then, that the chancellor for James Cardinal Gibbons wrote:

> "Of course the change of the day was her act. It could not have been otherwise, as no one in those days would have dreamed of doing anything in matters spiritual and ecclesiastical and religious without her. And the act is a mark of her ecclesiastical authority in religious things."[15]

---

14 Peter Geiermann, *The Convert's Catechism of Catholic Doctrine,* (St. Louis, Missouri: Herder Book Company, 1957) 50.

15 H. F. Thomas, letter, November 11, 1895, as quoted in *What Jesus Said,* 467.

Did you get it? The act, by her own admission, of changing the day from Saturday to Sunday is a mark of her authority in religious things. A "mark"—have we been looking for a mark?

"He causes all, both small and great, rich and poor, free and slave, to receive a mark on their right hand or on their foreheads, and that no one may buy or sell except one who has the mark or the name of the beast, or the number of his name." (Revelation 13:16, 17)

Need we say more? God warns us. The confession is made; the Catholic Church says, "We did it"—it is the mark of our authority.

The Bible says a time is coming when this edict will be enforced by boycott—unless you have a certain mark or designation, you are not going to be able to buy or sell. But it is a mark of apostasy, and the person who receives that mark incurs the wrath of God. Do you see why it is important for all the world to know the issues that are forthcoming? Do you see why I have said for so long that this is not simply a quarrel between two twenty-four-hour days of worship, but this, instead, is a matter of allegiance? Are we going to take a "thus saith the Lord," or are we going to put manmade tradition in place of the Word of God? I think you can see also why we have said that keeping the Sabbath is a matter of following Jesus when it comes to our attention.

This movement is not something being done in a corner. This is one of the greatest issues ever to grip the hearts of men and women, and it is going to get bigger. This is going to be a tremendously decisive issue in the last days. The day is rapidly approaching when manmade laws will bring this issue to a showdown. God, in His mercy, draws it to our attention before it happens so that we can know and prepare for it and fortify ourselves against the devil's deception.

What difference does it make what day I keep? May God help us to see that all eternity hangs in the balance because it is a matter of my allegiance either to Him or to an apostate power.

I am not saying that those who keep Sunday have the mark of the beast. The Bible does not teach that. But it does teach that when the decree enforcing the counterfeit Sabbath is given, those who do not take their stand on the side of right will naturally receive the mark of apostasy. So it is a matter of either worshiping the beast or worshiping "Him who made heaven and earth" (Revelation 14:7).

Do you see why right in the heart of this message, God distinguishes those who are victorious over the beast and his image as those who keep the commandments of God? Do you see how all this begins to fit together in a great mosaic and it all makes sense? It is the devil's clever design to lead us astray in our allegiance.

I want to be counted among the number of those who are faithful when Jesus comes. Furthermore, I want to be among that great company that is spreading that word now to all the world and warning men and women so that they will not be led astray.

Don't you?